"The recent revival of interest ir ... reated a need to provide modern reac ... it. The editors of *The 1662 Book of Common Prayer, International Edition* have assumed no prior knowledge of liturgical worship and have guided readers step by step through its principles and content. This book challenges both students and pastors to reflect carefully about our public devotion to the service of God and shows how it can be enriched by drawing on this classical English text."

Gerald Bray, research professor of divinity at Samford University

"Samuel Bray and Drew Nathaniel Keane have succeeded extraordinarily in a task where many others have failed. This introduction to the ascetical use of the Book of Common Prayer (for it has no other purpose!) is given a very helpful historical background that never overwhelms the purpose of the prayer book and this volume: to help us to pray, and to pray rightly. No single book of prayers has shaped the prayer lives of English speakers like the 1662 BCP, and thankfully this little guide will only add more names to that list."

Matthew S. C. Olver, publisher and executive director of The Living Church Foundation

"The Book of Common Prayer is the undisputed masterpiece of English liturgy that has stirred the souls of countless Anglicans (and others) across five centuries. This guide opens with a short history of the BCP and then expounds the significance of the components of the various services. Readers unfamiliar with the BCP will find it to be a treasure trove of public and private devotion to God, while those familiar with its use will be blessed by the careful explanation of the liturgical magnificence of Thomas Cranmer, the expert liturgist. This book will be a valuable resource for many."

Glenn N. Davies, former archbishop of Sydney

"This is a wonderful resource for helping modern people understand the theory and the nitty-gritty of Anglican liturgical prayers. It is simple, clear, and easy to read but full of profound insights into the history, theology, and practicalities of *The 1662 Book of Common Prayer, International Edition*. I warmly commend it!"

Lee Gatiss, director of Church Society and editor *of The First Book of Homilies: The Church of England's Official Sermons in Modern English*

"As a user and teacher of the Book of Common Prayer on the ground in local churches, I have long hoped for a resource like this to hit the shelves. For me and my congregations, it needed to be comprehensively researched, theologically tuned to Cranmer's intentions, and then written with a punchy immediacy that wonderfully ordinary worshipers could enjoy. Thank God that resource is finally here!"

Zac Hicks, pastor of Church of the Cross in Birmingham, Alabama, and author of *Worship by Faith Alone*

"I've been consistently blessed and also enlightened in reading and reflecting on the insights of this unique guidebook. It's much more than just a guide. Having been raised on prayer book worship, and then having led Anglican worship for fifty additional years, I am pretty well saturated with the prayers and poetry of the Book of Common Prayer, the unique book that nurtured Wesley, Whitefield, Newton, Stott, Packer, and millions more. Yet each chapter fed and refreshed me in my own walk with Christ. Reading Bray and Keane is like sitting with a wise, godly mentor who wants to open your mind and heart to new depths of worship."

John Yates, founding pastor of The Falls Church Anglican

"Samuel Bray and Drew Keane have put together a guide that will lead those unused to worship with the prayer book through the basics of the use of the Book of Common Prayer and beyond. The prayer book is presented here as a map through the Christian life in an Anglican key, with sections on daily prayer, the celebration of baptism, confirmation, and Communion, the shape of the liturgical year, the memorials of saints' days, and more. This lovely and straightforward book is remarkably precise and subtle in its theological formation of the one who gets hold of it and follows its trail into the heart of the liturgical life of the church."

Susannah Black Roberts, editor of *Plough* and *Breaking Ground: Charting Our Future in a Pandemic Year*

"*The 1662 Book of Common Prayer, International Edition* is a beautiful book that stands well in the line of ancient, medieval, and Reformation-era breviaries. Given that evangelical Christians today are largely unfamiliar with praying the Divine Office, the BCP's riches are lost on many. This is why the Herculean work of Bray and Keane is such a blessing to the church. Now they have provided us with a brilliant handbook that teaches us both how to use the BCP and the rich theological meaning of every detail of the services. Their manual is itself a source of spiritual devotion that fills the soul while helping us to pray!"

Ian Clary, associate professor of historical theology at Colorado Christian University

"This is a wonderfully clear and accessible guide, ably communicating the purpose of Christian liturgy, the rationale of the prayer book, and how it can be used most fruitfully. For any who are new to the Book of Common Prayer, this volume will serve to open a treasure to them; for those already familiar with it, it will deepen their understanding and appreciation."

Alastair Roberts, teaching fellow of the Davenant Institute and author of *Echoes of Exodus: Tracing Themes of Redemption Through Scripture*

How to Use the
Book of Common Prayer

A Guide to the Anglican Liturgy

Samuel L. Bray and
Drew Nathaniel Keane

An imprint of InterVarsity Press
Downers Grove, Illinois

InterVarsity Press
P.O. Box 1400 | Downers Grove, IL 60515-1426
ivpress.com | email@ivpress.com

InterVarsity Press® is the publishing division of InterVarsity Christian Fellowship/USA®. For more information, visit intervarsity.org.

All quotations and page citations from the Book of Common Prayer are from *The 1662 Book of Common Prayer: International Edition* (IVP Academic, 2021). All rights to new material and updated language reserved. Quotations from the Psalms are from the Book of Common Prayer. Quotations from Saint Augustine, John Boys, Thomas Comber, Thomas Cranmer, John Davenant, John Donne, Richard Hooker, John Jewel, Anthony Sparrow, James Ussher, and the two Books of Homilies are modernized by the authors.

Cover design: David Fassett
Interior design: Jeanna Wiggins
Cover image: Ornate title page of The Book of Common Prayer, 1844 / Library of Congress

ISBN 978-1-5140-0747-1 (print) | ISBN 978-1-5140-0748-8 (digital)

Printed in the United States of America ♾

Library of Congress Cataloging-in-Publication Data
Names: Bray, Samuel L., author. | Keane, Drew Nathaniel, 1987- author.
Title: How to use the Book of common prayer : a guide to the Anglican
   liturgy / Samuel L. Bray and Drew Nathaniel Keane.
Description: Downers Grove, IL : IVP Books, [2024] | Includes
   bibliographical references and index.
Identifiers: LCCN 2023037425 (print) | LCCN 2023037426 (ebook) | ISBN
   9781514007471 (print) | ISBN 9781514007488 (digital)
Subjects: LCSH: Church of England. Book of common prayer. | Church of
   England–Liturgy.
Classification: LCC BX5145 B699 2024 (print) | LCC BX5145 (ebook) | DDC
   264/.03–dc23/eng/20231025
LC record available at https://lccn.loc.gov/2023037425
LC ebook record available at https://lccn.loc.gov/2023037426

30 29 28 27 26 25 24 | 13 12 11 10 9 8 7 6 5 4 3 2 1

Contents

1

Liturgy?

✝

EACH WEEK, HUNDREDS OF MILLIONS of Christians all over the world go to church. There are some constants. In almost every church, Christians are praying, reading the Bible, hearing sermons, singing songs, and sometimes receiving the Lord's Supper. There are also differences. Some churches are more *liturgical*. That word can mean a lot of things, but we are using it to mean that the words said by the people and the minister (except for the sermon) are written down in advance, and the words usually don't change from service to service. When they do change, it happens on a fixed, predictable schedule. Liturgy is scripted, not improv.

Most Christians attend liturgical services. If you're Ethiopian Orthodox or Swedish Lutheran, if you're a Roman Catholic in Mongolia or an Anglican in Nigeria, then on a typical Sunday you almost certainly go to a liturgical service. That's been true for most Christians throughout history. But for several generations, many Protestant churches in the Western hemisphere have been running in a different direction. They emphasize novelty and spontaneity, and they are making a sharp turn toward technology-saturated worship. Meanwhile, in the last few years, there has been a growing interest among Protestants, especially among young evangelicals, in liturgical worship. That may be why you picked up this book.

These two trends are not a coincidence. If you are tired of always chasing something new, and of following celebrity pastors and worship leaders, then liturgical worship can offer you a path of peace, a distinctive rhythm for how to be taught by Christ and abide in him.

Different churches have different liturgical "scripts." Since the Reformation, the one that's been the most widely used and influential in English-speaking churches is the 1662 Book of Common Prayer. This book you are holding will walk you through the Book of Common Prayer, inviting you into these liturgies that have shaped the lives of so many millions of Christians—from Jane Austen to the martyrs of Uganda, from John Wesley to the martyrs of Papua New Guinea.

If you struggle to summon up the right emotions and words, these pages offer another way. Here is soil that's good for putting down roots. Here is a bench to sit down on and rest awhile—a place to stay put.

WHY LITURGY?

People are drawn to liturgy for varied reasons. And the reasons you're attracted to it may not be the same as the reasons you stick with it years later. After all, when you first participate in a liturgical service, you are learning what to do and might feel lost. You may even wonder what the point is. So here are eight reasons to be drawn to liturgy—and to stick with it.

First, liturgical prayers allow you to pray not only by yourself, but with other Christians. The culture of the postmodern West is intensely individualistic, and that atomism and isolation can carry over into our prayer lives. Liturgical prayers push us outside of ourselves. When we are praying liturgical prayers with other people, we are participants and not spectators. Even little children can participate because the consistency and repetition allow them to learn the prayers and say them before they're able to read.

Liturgical prayers connect us with other Christians— whether in the next pew or around the world, and through many centuries. This connection with the broader church is everywhere in the Book of Common Prayer. It contains many prayers from the Reformation, yet these usually go back further still, often back to at least the 600s. It also contains prayers and songs of praise that come from other Protestant churches and Greek churches. The creeds in the prayer book also unite us to each other and to the broader church. And the Lord's Prayer, the inheritance of all Christians, is the "signature tune" that appears at least once in every service.[1]

Second, liturgical prayers give us words to say when we have none. Everyone encounters grief, loss, and despair, and when we walk through the valley of the shadow of death

(Psalm 23:4), we need prayer more than ever. When we struggle to find the words to say, liturgical prayers can come to the rescue.

Samuel Johnson, the writer of the first English dictionary, found solace in the prayer book in times of inner turmoil. "The sonorous cadences, the elegant repetitions and antitheses, of [the Book of Common Prayer] may strike some as cold. [Dr.] Johnson, however, did not need his heart warmed, but rather his racing mind calmed. For him, and for many who have felt themselves at the mercy of chaotic forces from within or without, the style of the prayer book has healing powers. It provides equitable balance when we ourselves have none."[2]

Third, liturgical prayers allow us to say "Amen" with confidence. Our prayers say things about God. What we say should be true—but what if it isn't? Our prayers also ask God for things. These petitions might be wise, but they might not be (Psalm 106:15). Liturgical prayers can let us know that what is being prayed is theologically sound and prudent. Writing to an American correspondent, C. S. Lewis said: "*Ex tempore* public prayer has this difficulty: we don't know whether we can mentally join in it until we've heard it—it might be phoney or heretical. We are therefore called upon to carry on a *critical* and a *devotional* activity at the same moment: two things hardly compatible. The rigid form really sets our devotions *free*."[3] Lewis wasn't the first to raise this concern. Writing almost two thousand years ago, the apostle Paul told the church in Corinth that it was important to pray and sing with understanding. Otherwise, Paul wrote, if visitors from outside the congregation walked into a service, how would they "be able to say 'Amen' to your thanksgiving, since they do not know what you are saying?" (1 Corinthians 14:16 NIV).

Fourth, liturgy helps us remember that worship is serious business. We live in a democratic age, and we find it easy to be casual but struggle with formality and reverence. We have forgotten what it means to be a subject reverently approaching a king. But in worship, we approach the king of the universe, the holy and omnipotent God. To worship him means to offer what he is worth, to render to him what he is rightly due. As the psalmist says, "Give the LORD the honour due unto his name; worship the LORD with holy worship" (Psalm 29:2). The language of the liturgy is meant to be "thickened" language, with more body and depth than everyday language, but without being pompous or self-important (like the language of the Pharisee in Matthew 6:5). It's not easy to strike this balance of elevation and humility, but for Christian liturgy the model is the language of the Scriptures themselves—especially the language of the Psalms, which are quoted again and again in the prayers of Jesus and of Paul. When a liturgy adopts the model of the Psalms, we are approaching God in a way that he himself has taught us.

One of the ways that language is fuller and richer in liturgy is through the use of older language. In fact, from the time of Christ to the present, churches have tended to worship in language that is older than what is spoken in everyday settings. Early Christians who heard the Psalms in Hebrew would have heard a classical form of the language.

Saint Augustine preached from Greek versions of the Old Testament that were hundreds of years old. Saint Jerome's translation of the Bible into Latin, called the Vulgate, was not consciously archaic when produced. But it certainly became so during its use over the next thousand years in the Western church, and the Vulgate did not completely replace the older Latin translation in the liturgy. And the King James Version was intended to be old-fashioned on the day it was published.

There's nothing inherently valuable about archaic expressions. "Thou" is not better than "you"; "beginneth" isn't superior to "begins." But there are still good reasons for the tendency to be conservative about liturgical language. To start with, because God has revealed himself and taught us how to worship him, the church has tended to treasure biblical words rather than risk losing too much in translation. So, for example, Hebrew words like *amen* and *alleluia* were carried over into Greek liturgy, then into Latin, then into English.

Another reason is that approaching the Holy involves not only joy but also fear. The writer Annie Dillard put it this way: "I often think of the set pieces of liturgy as certain words which people have successfully addressed to God without their getting killed."[4] So there is a tendency to hand down and hold onto what we have learned through hard-won experience.

Another reason is that continuity turns our very words into a means for preserving the story of the church. The presence of the Greek *Kyrie eleison* (meaning "Lord, have mercy") in Latin liturgy, for example, preserved the memory of the early centuries when the underground church in Rome prayed and read the Scriptures in Greek. And keeping our liturgical language stable over time allows a rich network of connections to develop. Hymns can echo the liturgy, like the line from the *Te Deum* in Morning Prayer—"thou didst not abhor the Virgin's womb"—that is echoed in the Christmas carol "O Come, All Ye Faithful": "Lo, he abhors not the Virgin's womb." These allusions reverberate through our Bibles, liturgies, and hymns, like echoing voices in the stone vaults of a cathedral. Because this way of talking is associated with prayer, it signals to us what a special and sacred thing we are doing when we hear and say these words.

It is essential to understand the prayers we say and the passages we read, just like we need to understand the words we sing. But the language of the Book of Common Prayer is usually simple and straightforward, like John Newton's "'Tis grace hath brought me safe thus far, / And grace will lead me home." The challenge of the prayer book's language is usually not understanding it, but really meaning it. Of course the liturgy will and must change over time. Lewis thought that as the English language changed, the Book of Common Prayer needed to change, too—and he suggested that the right pace was for it to occur "imperceptibly; here a little and there a little; one obsolete word replaced in a century."[5]

Fifth, liturgy is a framework for hearing the word of God. In fact, we are never closer to the original setting of the Scriptures than when we hear them read in the liturgy. That's because the Scriptures were not originally written down for silent individual reading. By and large, they were written for public reading, usually in a worship setting and in cultures in which most people could not read and write, in order to prompt active response. Sometimes the biblical text even preserves the liturgy as a liturgy, with both the instructions and the words to say. An example is Deuteronomy 27:14-15 (NJPS):

> The Levites shall then proclaim in a loud voice to all the people of Israel:
>
> Cursed be any party who makes a sculptured or molten image, abhorred by the LORD, a craftsman's handiwork, and sets it up in secret.—And all the people shall respond, Amen.

So the Scriptures themselves show that liturgical worship is the natural setting for reading the Bible. And, by scripting appropriate responses to the Scriptures read aloud, liturgy shows us that God speaks in order to prompt action. His word is living and active; blessed are those who hear the word and obey (Hebrews 4:12; Luke 11:28).

Sixth, liturgical prayers offer protection for the laity. Clergy are human, after all, and that means it is easy to have favorite topics for prayer and preaching. What seems to the minister like a valuable emphasis can easily seem to the people like a private agenda or a hobbyhorse. Even when the prayers are written down, if they are not fixed but are changeable at the whim of the minister, the people may be subjected to innovations that are more eccentric than edifying. Jesus told the apostle Peter, "Feed my sheep" (John 21:17 KJV), not "experiment on my guinea pigs." Fixed liturgical prayers protect the laity from a constant churn of experimentation and even error.[6]

Seventh, the best liturgical prayers have a simple, sturdy beauty. God can hear and answer prayers in our own words (thank goodness!), but as those words tumble out, I might mutter things that are vague or circuitous—maybe distracted—with fits and starts and hesitations. I may want to ask God for something but be uncertain what to ask for. Maybe the words I say never fully amount to what I mean. Still, God knows. As one of the prayers in the Book of Common Prayer puts it, we are approaching "Almighty God, the fountain of all wisdom, who knowest our necessities before we ask and our ignorance in asking" (p. 267 in the 1662 International Edition). The words of liturgical prayers can be focused, concentrated, rich beyond what I can cobble together on the spot. Especially in public services, liturgical prayers help ensure that everything spoken will build up the whole congregation (1 Corinthians 14:4). And whether the prayers are spoken in public or private, these words, beyond our own ability to compose, can draw our hearts along a well-traveled path of devotion toward God.

Eighth, liturgical prayers can become inscribed in our memories. The prayers in the Book of Common Prayer effectively deploy repetition, rhythm, and other rhetorical devices.[7] These prayers come from a time when written and spoken English weren't so separate, when written English was written not just for the eye but for the ear, making it easier to memorize. We can learn these prayers by heart. We can say them while we are walking, bicycling, or driving. We can remember them when we sit with a dying friend. And what is learned by heart can be shared across the generations. Liturgical prayers are like great hymns, such as "Rock of Ages" and "O for a Thousand Tongues to Sing"—they express gospel truths, with words that etch themselves into the memory, words that connect father and son, grandmother and granddaughter. What we memorize and meditate on will change us, becoming part of who we are (Psalm 1:2-3).

To be sure, not all liturgical prayers are well-crafted. Some are disposable and will not be handed down from generation to generation. It's not clear whether the most recent batch of liturgical prayers, especially many written since the late twentieth century, will stand the test of time. But all eight of the reasons just given for using liturgy apply with full force to the classic Book of Common Prayer. It gives us words when we have none: words drenched in Scripture, reverent words, words that draw in old and young and that draw on the experience and wisdom of the broader church, words that are beautiful and memorable, trustworthy words.

WHAT ABOUT FREEDOM?

But liturgy can prompt questions, even objections. We all love freedom, and it's built into human nature that we do not like to be told what to do. Before today, there's probably never been another culture or era of human history where people so often praised individual freedom and choice. That presents a challenge for a book about liturgy. One of the first things you'll notice in the Book of Common Prayer is instructions printed in red (or in some editions, in italics). These instructions are called *rubrics*. As you turn the pages, you see more and more rubrics. It's almost like it's telling us, "Say *these* words, not some other words. Say *this* prayer, not some other prayer." These liturgical prayers that are written down in advance and not made up on the spot—do they constrain my freedom? Are these the "vain repetitions" (Matthew 6:7 KJV) that Jesus warned us about?

The pattern in the Bible might surprise you. When Jesus taught his disciples about prayer, he started with how to pray. Don't call attention to yourself; mean what you say; trust your Father in heaven (Matthew 6:5-8). But what did Jesus do next? He didn't give his disciples advice about the best structure for prayer. He gave them something even more useful: specific words to remember and use. "This, then, is how you should pray" (Matthew 6:9 NIV). And in the early church, the apostles followed this example of liturgical prayer. They said "the prayers" (Acts 2:42 RSV), which were likely liturgical prayers. We don't know what exactly these prayers were, but plausible guesses include psalms, familiar Jewish prayers, and the Lord's Prayer.[8] And the apostles prayed at regular times of the day, whether at the temple in Jerusalem or away from it (Acts 3:1, 10:9).

Following these examples, Christians have always used liturgical forms for prayer, while also recognizing a place outside of the liturgy for spontaneous prayers. In the first centuries after Christ, fixed forms of prayer developed across the Christian world. The church year began to take shape in the first two hundred years after Jesus' birth, and in different places there were settled patterns for how the sacraments of baptism and the Lord's Supper were celebrated. In both Eastern and Western churches, liturgical forms were the norm for public worship in the first fifteen hundred years after Christ.

That continued with the Reformation. It may be surprising to many Protestants today, but Martin Luther's Wittenberg and John Calvin's Geneva had liturgical forms for prayer and for the sacraments. The Protestant Reformation was about liturgy just as much as it was about doctrine, but it was not a rejection of liturgy. In fact, the reformers insisted on liturgy.[9] But they wanted a liturgy that was not in Latin, so the people could understand it; a liturgy purged of corruptions; a liturgy that taught the people the word of God.

Of course, our hearts need to be in the prayers we say, and it is not enough just to recite the words. The liturgy does not work by osmosis; it does not form us as Christians automatically. The same is true for hymns and songs in worship. It is not enough just to sing the words without meaning them. Yet there are still many advantages to having hymns composed before a service instead of being made up on the spot—advantages like greater participation, assurance of doctrinal soundness, and compelling and memorable words. More than that, singing familiar hymns again and again actually enhances rather than diminishes their capacity to express the inarticulate longings of our hearts.[10] If we can sing hymns written down in advance, without thinking that makes them fake or insincere, why not say prayers written down in advance?[11]

The idea that liturgical prayers are in conflict with prayer from the heart, with really meaning what we say, is relatively new in Christian history. Jesus, the apostles, churches before and after the Reformation—all used fixed forms of liturgical prayer. For most of the last two thousand years, Christians have used liturgical prayers *and* spontaneous prayers, with liturgical prayers predominating in public worship and adding richness and depth to the spontaneous prayers used in private worship. This Christian tradition of liturgical prayer is carried on in the Book of Common Prayer, which we will explore in the chapters that follow.

2

A Ten-Minute History of the Prayer Book

✚

THE ORIGINS OF THE BOOK of Common Prayer lie in the sixteenth century, in the upheaval of the Reformation. In the early 1500s, Europe was stirring. In 1516, the Dutch scholar Erasmus published the first fresh Latin translation of the Scriptures in a millennium. In 1517, Martin Luther published his 95 Theses, denouncing the selling of indulgences that were supposed to free the buyers' loved ones from purgatory. In 1522, Huldrych Zwingli served sausages during Lent, arguing that Christian fasting should be voluntary.

Throughout the lands of the Holy Roman Empire, including areas that are now Germany, France, and Switzerland, reformers called the church back to the authority of the Scriptures and insisted that we are pardoned from sin solely on the basis of faith in Christ. In these reforming churches—labels like "Protestant," "Lutheran," and "Calvinist" were not used yet, but would come soon—there was a new emphasis on the people hearing God's word in their own language. But even while the Reformation was beginning on the Continent, the situation was different in England.

During the 1530s there were striking changes to the English church. King Henry VIII and Parliament abolished the jurisdiction of the Roman pope and dissolved the monasteries, toppling two pillars of the medieval religious superstructure. But for the typical English lay person, the experience of worship barely changed. Many lay people attended weekly or even daily Mass, yet much of the service was inaudible to them. And it was in Latin, so even when the people could hear, they usually couldn't understand. Lay people attending church would say their own private prayers until the ringing of a bell directed their attention toward the priest, who was lifting into the air what appeared to be a wafer—but was believed to be not bread but something else entirely, the very body of Christ, presented anew to God as a sacrifice for the sins of the faithful, both the living and the dead. Usually only the clergy received, and when the laity did, the chalice was withheld from them. No matter how deeply moving the service was for lay people—and for many it certainly was—the sense of exclusion was unmistakable. The readings were not in their language, the prayers were not in their ears, the service books were not in their hands, and the chalice never touched their lips.

But change was coming. King Henry VIII was succeeded in 1547 by his nine-year-old son, Edward VI, opening the door to full-scale religious reform.

✢ ✢ ✢

ARCHBISHOP CRANMER'S ACHIEVEMENT

June 9, 1549, was a Sunday. It was Pentecost, or as it was known in England, Whitsunday. This was the day that the archbishop of Canterbury selected as the first Sunday when the new Book of Common Prayer would be used in services all through the land of England. That archbishop was Thomas Cranmer, godfather of Edward VI and of the English Reformation.

Archbishop Cranmer's selection of Whitsunday was not an accident. The second chapter of Acts records that on the day of Pentecost, as the apostles spoke, each person heard the word of God "in his own language" (Acts 2:6 RSV). Now, for the first time, all through the land, those who spoke English would hear the word of God in their own language. Now, instead of a daily Mass that was said on behalf of the people—and in Latin, so even if they attended and were able to hear the largely inaudible words, they could not understand them—there would be daily services of Morning and Evening Prayer in which the people heard and understood the word of God.

The book first used on that day has turned out to be something beyond what anyone at the time could have imagined. After the Bible, the Book of Common Prayer has been the most widely used book in the English language. By one scholar's count, "Up to a billion people have said prayers together, got married, or buried their families and friends, saying its words."[1]

But none of that was known in 1548 and early 1549, when Archbishop Cranmer sat in his library at Lambeth Palace, surrounded by books. He had gathered what was probably the largest collection of liturgical texts in Europe, and from them he was compiling—probably with help from a supporting cast—the first Book of Common Prayer. His main sources were the Latin service books used in the English church. Many of the prayers in these books had been in use in the Western Church for at least eight hundred years, and Cranmer translated them into clear, dignified English. Other prayers were drawn from the work of reformers on the Continent, or from liturgies of the Greek churches. And still others were original compositions, either by Cranmer or colleagues working with him.

We can see Cranmer's consummate liturgical craftsmanship in the way he wove these varied threads into a single coherent whole. The language of the Book of Common Prayer is euphonious and memorable, and it stands up under the test of constant repetition. There is something paradoxical about this language. It is plain, not ornate. Yet it is also beautiful. It is emotionally restrained, yet deeply moving. It conveys intimacy as well as grandeur; human warmth, but also a note of reverence and awe, of transcendence.

Sometimes people compare the language of the Book of Common Prayer to William Shakespeare, but it's much simpler and homelier. Its "cadences have the grace of strength rather than of decoration."[2] The prayer book is sometimes called "poetic," but none of it is actually verse. In fact, Cranmer was a mediocre poet, and he knew it. The gift he had was in writing the kind of liturgical English that can be used day in, day out, without ever becoming trite. Cranmer also had a sense of drama. He knew how to build a service to a crescendo, and how to strip away verbal and ceremonial distractions so that the words and ceremonies that remained would have unevadable force.

Cranmer and the other English reformers would have been appalled at the idea that they were producing "great literature." Their language bears the weight of conviction, and their goal was to turn the kingdom of England toward repentance, and toward sincere and genuine faith. Their chief means of doing that was to ensure that the people would know the life-giving Scriptures: "So then faith cometh by hearing, and hearing by the word of God" (Romans 10:17 KJV). As Alan Jacobs wrote, "Cranmer's book, and its direct successors, will always be acknowledged as historical documents of the first order, and masterpieces of English prose, but that is not what they want or mean to be. Their goal—now as in 1549—is to be living words in the mouths of those who have a living faith."[3]

That is why Cranmer made sure that every service in the Book of Common Prayer proclaims the gospel—the good news that sinners can be pardoned and saved because of the death of Christ. The prayer book is designed to proclaim the gospel persuasively. It manages the hearers' encounter with the divine word in several ways: first using the Scriptures to prompt self-examination in order to hammer away at our hard hearts; then using the Scriptures to offer broken and contrite hearts the balm of the gospel; and finally using the Scriptures to point faithful hearts to appropriate ways of responding to the gospel (such as praise, prayer, good works, almsgiving, and feasting at the Lord's table). Cranmer made sure every service is filled with Scripture, and almost 80 percent of the Book of Common Prayer is from the Bible. "The Prayer Book['s] . . . liturgy is not an alternative to being Word-centered, but rather a way of being so."[4]

In this aim, Cranmer was working closely with leaders in the Reformed and Lutheran churches on the Continent. Like them, he was always careful to follow and teach the catholic doctrine of the creeds, including the doctrines of the Trinity and incarnation. All three creeds of the Western church are included in the Book of Common Prayer and are said regularly: the Apostles' Creed, the Nicene Creed, and the Athanasian Creed. Yet he was also careful to prune away medieval accretions like prayers to the saints, purgatory, transubstantiation, and the practice of offering the Mass to God as a sacrifice for sin. In place of these doctrines, the Book of Common Prayer emphasizes that Jesus Christ is the only mediator between God and man, that we are justified by faith alone, and that the believer feeds on Christ in the sacrament "after a heavenly and spiritual manner" (Article 28, which is in the 1662 International Edition at p. 640).

But the English reformers were concerned with more than beauty and truth. They were also concerned with simplicity, or what we might call usability. In Cranmer's preface to the Book of Common Prayer, called "Concerning the Service of the Church," he has two main complaints about the late medieval services. One is that they were in Latin, which the people couldn't understand. The other is that they were too complicated. As he memorably put it, because of "the number and hardness of the rules" and "the manifold changings of the service, . . . there was more business to find out what should be read, than to read it when it was found out" (p. xv).

These themes—the gospel, thoroughly catholic and thoroughly reformed doctrine, simplicity, and beauty—are key to understanding the Book of Common Prayer. Previously there had been many books and they had been in Latin, unintelligible to the laity. Now everything was in one book, for clergy and laity, for churches and homes. It was a book of prayer for everyone to hold in common.

REVISION AND REVOLUTION

The first Book of Common Prayer was published in 1549, but it was not the last. The English reformers had been cautious; in the first edition they had not moved as far as they wanted to. And the reaction to the new Book of Common Prayer showed that some parts were ambiguous, especially about whether the prayer book decisively rejected transubstantiation. Transubstantiation is the teaching that the "substances" of bread and wine are miraculously replaced through the consecration prayer with the flesh and blood of Jesus Christ.

In 1552, Archbishop Cranmer produced a revised edition. Although the theology of the Book of Common Prayer was not greatly changed, it was articulated more clearly. The Holy Communion service was streamlined and ambiguities were removed: now there was no way it could be interpreted as the priest offering Jesus Christ as a sacrifice to God for sin, and those receiving communion were now told to "feed on him in thy heart by faith." A new introduction with confession and absolution was added to the daily services, and all prayers for the dead were removed from the burial service. It was a clearer, better organized prayer book.

As this new edition of the Book of Common Prayer was used throughout England—common prayer for the whole kingdom—it seemed like the English Reformation would finally take root. But that appearance was deceptive. The next year, 1553, the young king, Edward VI, died. He was succeeded by his half sister, Queen Mary I, who banned the Book of Common Prayer and restored the Latin Mass. She persecuted the reformers—earning the nickname "Bloody Mary"—and among the more than three hundred Reformation martyrs executed by Mary would be Archbishop Cranmer himself, who in 1556 at age sixty-five was burned alive at the stake, condemned in part for the doctrine and worship of the prayer book.

But Queen Mary's reign did not last long. In 1558, she too died and was succeeded by her half sister Queen Elizabeth I. For the people of England, it was the third coronation of a monarch in about a decade, and each new monarch had brought a decisive shift in worship. Queen

Elizabeth appointed new bishops, including Protestant reformers—like John Jewel—who had been exiles on the Continent during Queen Mary's rule.

Under Queen Elizabeth, the revised Book of Common Prayer was restored, with only a few adjustments. One change was to the words the priest said when he gave the bread and wine to each communicant. In Queen Elizabeth's 1559 edition of the prayer book, the words from the 1549 edition of the Book of Common Prayer ("The body of our Lord Jesus Christ, which was given for thee, preserve thy body and soul unto everlasting life") were combined with the words from the 1552 edition ("Take and eat this in remembrance that Christ died for thee, and feed on him in thy heart by faith with thanksgiving"). The 1559 adjustments do not seem to have caused any controversy. Then, in 1561, the calendar was altered and special Old Testament readings for Sundays were added.

Over the next century, there would be almost no change in the Book of Common Prayer. One small change was the addition to the catechism of a new section on the sacraments (1604). And people began adding to the back of the Book of Common Prayer things that had previously been printed as separate books—including the Psalter, the Articles of Religion (the Anglican doctrinal statement), and the Ordinal (the services for ordaining clergy). But there was essentially no change to the prayer book itself.

During the English Civil War in the 1640s, the Book of Common Prayer was once again banned—this time, not by a Catholic queen but by a Puritan Parliament. After the Civil

War passed and Oliver Cromwell died, a weary nation welcomed back a new king, Charles II. He brought back the prayer book, which had been illegal to use in church for nearly two decades. During that time, it had been treasured by many people throughout England, who continued to privately say its prayers and read its psalms.

When the Book of Common Prayer was restored, it was also revised. For the new 1662 edition, every page was scrutinized. The larger changes made were (1) using the King James Version for the readings from the epistles and gospels, (2) adding a service of Holy Baptism for adults, (3) adding special prayers for use at sea, and (4) making the Psalter, which had always been used with the Book of Common Prayer, part of the book itself.

There were many small refinements as well. For example, there were new prayers for those preparing for ordination, special psalms for Good Friday, and instructions about consuming any remaining consecrated bread and wine after a service of Holy Communion. Nevertheless, as one liturgical scholar has observed, "in the end it is the same book that emerges with only minor alterations."[5]

Much had changed in the century between 1552 and 1662. In 1552, England was a small kingdom on the periphery of Europe, hardly a great power, with a frail fourteen-year old king and a tenuous commitment to the Protestant Reformation. In 1662, it had a restored monarchy, as well as the confidence of a kingdom whose authors now included Spenser and Shakespeare. The Royal Navy patrolled the sea lanes connecting London with colonies that stretched from

Massachusetts to Jamaica. England was now the leading Protestant country in the world.

But through all these changes, the Book of Common Prayer was substantially the same, and by 1662 several generations of English men and women had been baptized, married, and buried by ministers who said its words.

THE 1662 BOOK OF COMMON PRAYER TODAY

The 1662 Book of Common Prayer quickly spread around the world. It was the liturgy of the Church of England, and wherever the British empire spread, its services followed. The prayer book was used by settlers in Australia, sailors in California, and newly baptized Christians in Nigeria. It was translated into more than one hundred languages, from Arabic (1674) to Zulu (1882).

In the 1800s, the relationship of the Church of England to its daughter churches around the world began to change. In time, the different national churches became independent, with their own constitutions and bishops, but most continued to use the 1662 Book of Common Prayer. An early exception was America following the revolution. The newly organized Protestant Episcopal Church in the United States of America revised the prayer book, not least to replace prayers for King George III's victory over his enemies.[6] In 1878, the Church of Ireland modestly revised the prayer book as well. Then, in the twentieth century, more Anglican national churches began to adopt their own revisions of the Book of Common Prayer, with increasing divergence from the original.

Nevertheless, the 1662 Book of Common Prayer has a unique place. The reformation of the Church of England was advanced through a variety of texts that came to be called her "formularies," and these, in turn, have shaped the wider Anglican tradition beyond the Church of England. The 1662 Book of Common Prayer is one of these formularies. Another is the Articles of Religion, also called the Thirty-Nine Articles. The Articles are the Anglican doctrinal statement, or "theological identity-card," to borrow a phrase from J. I. Packer.[7] Still another formulary is the Ordinal, which contains the services for ordaining bishops, priests, and deacons. The Ordinal spells out the doctrine of ministry, including the role of bishops. There are also two Books of Homilies, which explain key doctrines in sermon form. (We discuss the Books of Homilies in chapter ten.) It's standard practice for a printing of the 1662 Book of Common Prayer to include the Articles and the Ordinal at the back, and the International Edition also includes one of the homilies (at p. 654).

The 1662 Book of Common Prayer is used to this day. It remains the official prayer book of the Church of England and is supported by the Prayer Book Society. Around the world there are many churches, schools, and individuals who use it.[8] In most Anglican churches, even where the 1662 Book of Common Prayer is not used in a typical worship service, it continues along with the other formularies to be a standard for Anglican belief and worship.[9] Yet there are some impediments to using the 1662 Prayer Book, especially because the prayers for civil authorities are so closely and explicitly tied to the British monarch and the royal family. Our aim in editing the 1662 International Edition was to remove these impediments.

When Cranmer and his associates first compiled the Book of Common Prayer and published it for use in English churches on Whitsunday in 1549, no one could have imagined that its words would echo through so many centuries and so many places. Yet the words of the Book of Common Prayer and, most of all, the words of the Scriptures that are contained in the book, have nourished the faith of hundreds of millions of Christians. They continue to do so, as the 1662 Book of Common Prayer is rediscovered by a new generation of those who want common prayer. What is it about the prayer book that has sustained the souls and captured the imaginations of so many people? That question is answered by the rest of this book.

3

The Ascent of Morning and Evening Prayer

✝

THE HEART OF THE BOOK of Common Prayer is the daily offices—Morning Prayer and Evening Prayer. These services nourish your soul, but not with intense bursts of devotion or with a dizzying complex of options that let you customize your devotional experience. They offer something else: simplicity, structure, Scripture.

Over the last five hundred years, Morning and Evening Prayer have been the most widely and frequently used Christian services in the English language. Unlike the services of Holy Baptism and Holy Communion, Morning and Evening Prayer do not require an ordained minister. They are for everyone. Although these services are designed to be said in a group, you can say them by yourself. All you need is a Bible and a Book of Common Prayer. All you have to do is show up ready to hear God's word, and to walk along a path of prayer that is already laid out for you. Each service will take you about half an hour. It can be a little longer depending on the day's readings, or if you're new to it.

Morning and Evening Prayer have two aims. First, they are meant to help us read the Bible—not just skimming our eyes across the page, but reading deeply for the good of our souls. Second, they help us respond to the Scriptures with gratitude, offering ourselves to God as living sacrifices (see Romans 6:19; 12:1).

If we keep those two aims in mind, we can better understand how Archbishop Cranmer designed these services. He drew on the ancient pattern of monastic prayer, comprising eight services at fixed times of day: Mattins, Lauds, and Prime in the morning; Terce, Sext, and None in the middle of the day; and Vespers and Compline in the evening. Cranmer streamlined those services so they could be used by all Christians. Everything he retained for these two services of Morning and Evening Prayer is meant to ensure that we approach the Scriptures with repentance and faith, and that we offer ourselves to God in prayer and thanksgiving.

Each service has four parts: *preparing, praising, hearing,* and *praying.* The last three are designed to draw us nearer to God. But because our sinfulness gets in the way of these means of drawing near to God, as the service begins we acknowledge our sin and express our desire for true repentance.

There are some small variations between the services of Morning and Evening Prayer, but the basic structure is the same, and most of the prayers are identical. Once you've learned one of these services, you know both of them.

As we move along the path provided by Morning or Evening Prayer, there is a clear trajectory. As the service begins, we come to God as sinners who need his forgiveness and grace. As the service ends, we find ourselves in a very different place. We have been assured of God's forgiveness and have responded with praise; we have heard the Holy Scriptures; we have brought our petitions to our heavenly Father. The final notes are grace and peace.

In these services, we are treading a path of spiritual ascent. It's a path that millions of other Christians have taken day after day for centuries. Taking this path, we are joining with the church in praise and prayer.

THE RED AND THE BLACK

Your copy of the Book of Common Prayer probably has some words in red and some in black. The red words, the *rubrics* (from the Latin word for red), are the instructions. In some printings, the rubrics are in italics instead of red. Read the rubrics silently, and once you've learned the service, you won't even need to read them anymore. The black words are said aloud (except headings and citations).

One of the main things the rubrics indicate is who is supposed to speak. They refer to the "minister" or "priest." Those terms are used interchangeably in Morning and Evening Prayer, and both words come from the New Testament. *Minister* means "servant," a word Jesus and the apostle Paul frequently used to refer to the church's leaders.

Priest comes to English from the Greek word *presbyteros*, which means "elder," another word used by the apostles to refer to church leaders. The rubrics also refer to the "people" or "congregation," and these terms are interchangeable.

If you are saying Morning or Evening Prayer in a group, whoever is leading the group says the words assigned to the minister/priest. If you are saying Morning or Evening Prayer by yourself, you say all the words, including those assigned to the minister/priest and those assigned to people/congregation. Some words are said by everyone together.

A Step-by-Step Guide

1. Preparing

The first part of Morning and Evening Prayer is *preparing*, but you may be in for a surprise. You may be used to services starting with a call to worship, but that's not how these services begin. Before we can even be called to worship, something has to be addressed: sin. This is a deeply biblical idea, the idea that before we worship we need forgiveness and cleansing (Exodus 19 and 40; Isaiah 6). The Book of Common Prayer ensures this preparation for worship in seven steps:

- sentences
- exhortation
- confession
- absolution
- Lord's Prayer

- short responsive prayers
- psalm of invitation and warning (Morning Prayer)

The first of these steps is the "sentences of the Scriptures" (pp. 1, 17 in the 1662 International Edition). These short quotations from the Bible are meant to prime our hearts for full disclosure to God. They encourage us to be honest. They offer us a vision of true repentance—not something external, just going through the motions—but "a broken and contrite heart" (Psalm 51:17). They assure us that if we confess from the heart, our heavenly Father is "faithful and just to forgive us our sins" (1 John 1:9).

The person leading the service picks two or three sentences and reads them with "a loud voice" (pp. 1, 17). That simply means to read them so they can be heard by everyone—in line with the reformers' emphasis on all the people hearing the word of God.

Following the sentences is the "exhortation" (pp. 2, 18). It begins "Dearly beloved brethren, the Scripture moveth us in sundry places"—those places are the sentences just read—"to acknowledge and confess our manifold sins and wickedness." The exhortation encourages sincere, genuine repentance, and it outlines the major themes for the service: thanksgiving, praise, hearing the word of God, and petitionary prayer.

To help us confess our sins, the service provides a scripted confession (pp. 3, 19). The rubric calls it "the general confession" because it's not a confession of some particular sin, but rather a confession for every kind of sin—action and inaction, against God and against neighbor. At least sixteen different Bible verses are quoted or paraphrased in the general confession: Isaiah 53:6; Psalm 119:176; 1 Peter 2:25; Proverbs 19:21; Jeremiah 18:12; 2 Chronicles 28:13; Matthew 23:23; Psalm 38:3; Luke 18:13; Psalm 51:1; Nehemiah 13:22; Psalm 51:12; Romans 15:8; 1 John 2:12; Titus 2:11-12; John 14:13. The capital letters that start each line of this prayer indicate where the minister and people are supposed to pause for breath. (This capitalization practice is used throughout the Book of Common Prayer for texts said by the people.)

In the first half of the general confession we descend step by step into the depths of sin until we hit bottom with "And there is no health in us." There is no hedging or qualification. It is a radical admission that we are sick, and that to find healing we must look outside ourselves. The next word, "But," signals a shift from human failure to divine intervention (like in Ephesians 2:4).

You might notice the phrase *miserable offenders.* You might even be uncomfortable saying it. But as C. S. Lewis noted, the prayer book is not talking about our feelings; instead

it is using the word "miserable" in the old sense— meaning an object of pity. That a person can be a proper object of pity when he is not feeling miserable, you can easily understand if you imagine yourself looking down from a height on two crowded express trains that are traveling toward one another along the same line at 60 miles an hour. You can see that in forty seconds there will be a head-on collision. I think it would be very natural to say about the passengers of these trains, that they were objects of pity. This would not mean that they felt miserable themselves; but they would certainly be proper objects of pity. I think that is the sense in which to take the word "miserable." The Prayer Book does not mean that we should feel miserable but that if we could see things from a sufficient height above we should all realize that we are in fact proper objects of pity.[1]

After we have been honest and admitted to God our sinfulness and helplessness, the minister declares the gospel, stating the terms of forgiveness and offering hope and assurance to all those who turn from sin and cling to Christ Jesus. This is called the "absolution" (pp. 3, 19). Like the confession, it quotes or paraphrases a number of passages of Scripture, such as the teaching of the prophet Ezekiel that God desires for sinners to repent and live (Ezekiel 18:23).

Note that some think only a priest can say the absolution. Others think that when a priest isn't present, the absolution in Morning and Evening Prayer may be said by a deacon or lay person. The arguments are somewhat technical. We think the better view is that when a priest is not present, this form of absolution can be said by anyone, because it simply announces the good news of the forgiveness of sin.[2] Even if you agree (and you may not!) that anyone can proclaim the gospel with these words, the absolution should be read by an ordained minister if one is present, because proclaiming the gospel is the task for which ministers of the church are set apart (Mark 16:14-18; Acts 20:24; 2 Timothy 4:1-2).

The forgiveness declared in the absolution is for those who "truly repent" and "unfeignedly believe." We may find ourselves wondering: Is my contrition deep enough? Are my intentions pure enough? Is my will strong enough? If we're honest with ourselves, the answer is no (see Article 9, pp. 631-632). So the absolution turns us away from ourselves to seek "true repentance" from God. For he is the giver of "every good and perfect gift" (James 1:17 NIV), and repentance and the forgiveness of sins are among the gifts given by the exalted Christ (Acts 5:31). This forgiveness is for "true penitents who can say, 'Lord, I believe, help Thou mine unbelief.'"[3]

At this point, having confessed our sins from the heart and received an assurance of divine pardon, we are almost done with the preparation part of the service. Next is the Lord's Prayer (pp. 4, 20), the first of two times it is said in Morning or Evening Prayer. Each time we say the Lord's Prayer in the Book of Common Prayer, the emphasis falls on a different aspect of the prayer. Here, because we have just been assured of God's love and turned to him in repentance, we address him as "our Father." As we say the Lord's Prayer here, we are also looking forward to the appointed psalms because when we say them, we will be asking God to align our desires and purposes with his own: "Thy kingdom come. Thy will be done."

Next is a series of short prayers that work as a dialogue between the leader and the other participants (pp. 4, 20). Each pair of lines is taken from the Psalms, except the third pair, beginning "Glory be to the Father." Those two lines are a hymn called the *Gloria Patri* (pronounced *GLOH-ree-uh PAH-tree*) that has been used in Christian worship since ancient times. These short lines express our need for God's prevenient grace, that is, divine grace that precedes human will or action: God must open our lips, and only then can we praise him.

In Morning Prayer there is one more element of preparation: the recitation of Psalm 95. It is called the *Venite* after its first word in Latin, which means "O come," and you can pronounce it either *veh-NYE-tee* or *veh-NEE-teh*. This psalm exhorts us to praise, to pray, and to hear. These very activities will be the content of the rest of the service.

In part the *Venite* is a call to worship: "O come, let us sing"; "O come, let us worship and fall down." But it is more than that. It is a plea to hear the word of God, along with a warning about how *not* to hear the word of God. Merely comprehending the words is not enough. To truly hear God's voice is to be transformed. That will not happen, the Scriptures tell us, if we hear with hardened, proud hearts (compare Jeremiah 6:10; Matthew 13:13-14; 1 Peter 2:1-12). "Harden not your hearts" is a warning that we should not forget the disposition of humility described in the opening sentences and general confession. And in teaching this lesson, the *Venite* reminds us of the Exodus, when the people of Israel went through the waters and were liberated from slavery. Even after their deliverance, the Israelites faced a divine test in the wilderness, the challenge of responding properly to the divine voice. In this way, the *Venite* places us into the story of the Exodus and reminds us of the stakes whenever we hear the word of God.

2. *Praising*

The Psalter has been integral to Jewish and Christian devotions for millennia, and is an important part of the daily offices. Regular Morning and Evening Prayer will lead you through the entire Psalter in the course of a month, and you can find the psalms appointed for each morning and evening beginning on page 362. You can also chant the psalms, as discussed in chapter ten.

The Psalms printed in the Book of Common Prayer are from a translation by Miles Coverdale that was completed in 1540. Coverdale was the first person to publish a complete translation of the Bible in English. He incorporated much of the work of William Tyndale, who had already translated most of the Bible, and who was forced into exile and hiding, eventually suffering a martyr's death for the "crime" of translating the Bible.

During Henry VIII's reign, Coverdale twice fled to the Continent. With the accession of Edward VI in 1547, Coverdale returned and was made Bishop of Exeter. But only a few years later, under Mary, he was deprived of his bishopric, imprisoned, and then exiled. In exile he helped produce the Geneva Bible, an early and very widely used English translation. When Elizabeth became queen, Coverdale returned to England a venerable old reformer, taking up the rectorship of Saint Magnus the Martyr near London Bridge.

Coverdale had a gift for the English language that has rarely been rivaled. Even though Coverdale's version of the Psalms is technically prose, it has often been called poetic. The poet W. H. Auden said, "All I know is that Coverdale reads like poetry, and the modern versions don't."[4] C. S. Lewis went even further in his praise for Coverdale: "In beauty, in poetry, he, and St. Jerome, the great Latin translator, are beyond all whom I know."[5] Another writer, Ernest Clapton, discerned the secret of Coverdale's success in a combination that has eluded other English translators of the Psalms: "The tenderness, the soothing touch, the dignity and the majesty of Coverdale's version."[6]

The Psalms in the Book of Common Prayer are not only some of the most moving and evocative words in the English language (though they are that). They're also medicine for our souls. Saint Athanasius, an early bishop of Alexandria, once said of the Book of Psalms that in it "you learn about *yourself*. You find depicted in it all the movements of your soul, all its changes, its ups and downs, its failures and re-coveries. Moreover, whatever your particular need or trouble, from this same book you can select a form of words to fit it, so that you do not merely hear and then pass on, but learn the way to remedy your ill."[7]

Twelve and a half centuries later, the great English theologian Richard Hooker expanded on this theme. "What is there necessary for man to know which the Psalms are not able to teach?," asked Hooker. It is all here: "Heroical magnanimity, exquisite justice, grave moderation, exact wisdom, repentance unfeigned, unwearied patience, the mysteries of

God, the sufferings of Christ, the terrors of wrath, the comforts of grace, the works of Providence over this world and the promised joys of that world which is to come, all good necessarily to be either known or done or had, this one celestial fountain yieldeth."[8]

All this reading from the Book of Psalms makes Morning and Evening Prayer some of the most joyful services ever written. This isn't a flighty happiness. The Psalms are realistic about the intense suffering that marks this life. "I am clean forgotten, as a dead man out of mind; I am become like a broken vessel" (Psalm 31:12). "For my days are consumed away like smoke, and my bones are burnt up as it were a firebrand. My heart is smitten down and withered like grass, so that I forget to eat my bread" (Psalm 102:3-4).

Amid suffering, the Psalms teach us hard-won wisdom and a deeper delight. Yes, "heaviness may endure for a night, but joy cometh in the morning" (Psalm 30:5). One way the Psalms do this is by taking truths about God and ourselves and putting them into the first person. "But my trust is in thy mercy, and my heart is joyful in thy salvation" (Psalm 13:5). "The LORD is my shepherd; therefore can I lack nothing" (Psalm 23:1). As we say these words with our lips, we make them our own. We are orienting our hearts toward these truths; we are signing up for what we say.[9]

After each psalm, as a conclusion, the *Gloria Patri* is sung or said (p. 6). It is a reminder that each psalm—whether lament or thanksgiving, whether instruction or memory—is being read to the praise and glory of the Triune God. And because the Psalms are read as Christian

Scripture, they speak of Christ and of his church. Repeating the *Gloria Patri* at the end of each psalm also means that no matter what its individual focus, it is turned into a song of praise. Whatever our circumstances, the Lord's name is to be praised (Job 1:21).

How do you say the psalms in a group? The leader says the odd-numbered verses, and the other participants respond with the even-numbered verses. (Or one side of the room says the odd verses, and the other side says the even verses.) The *Gloria Patri* is said responsively, too, or it can be sung by the leader and the other participants together. If you're saying Morning or Evening Prayer by yourself, simply read the psalms and after each one say or sing the *Gloria Patri*.

3. Hearing

Now we're ready to hear and respond to God's word. Of course we just read the appointed psalms, and they're Scripture. But in Morning and Evening Prayer, the psalms aren't presented as "Bible readings," but as hymns of praise and turning to God, which is why they are sung or spoken responsively. In the psalms, we enter into conversation with God, both hearing his word and responding to him with the words that he gives us. The psalms prepare us to hear and respond to the other Scriptures as God's word.

This next part of Morning or Evening Prayer has five elements. Two of these elements are "lessons," or readings (p. 754). The other three elements are responses to the lessons. The first lesson is usually a chapter from the Old Testament, though sometimes it is from the Apocrypha.

The second lesson is from the New Testament. (For more on the lessons, including why the Apocrypha is read, see chapter seven.)

You can find the lessons by looking at the tables and calendar at the front of the prayer book. The tables give lessons for certain special days, but first look at the calendar, which is used day in and day out. Turn to page xxxiv, and if the current month is not January, keep going until you find the right month. The left-hand page is for "Mattins" (Morning Prayer), while the right-hand page is for "Evensong" (Evening Prayer). Look at the left-hand page and find the day of the month. The column titled "1 Lesson" gives you the first reading, and the column titled "2 Lesson" gives you the second reading. If you aren't sure what the abbreviation for the name of the book means, there is a table of abbreviations on page xxviii.

The text of the lessons isn't printed in the Book of Common Prayer, so you will need to read them from your own Bible. Two translations that match the language of the Book of Common Prayer more closely are the King James Version and the Revised Standard Version, but you can use any Bible you want.

The lessons are central to Morning and Evening Prayer. We could even think of these services as frameworks for reading the Bible. They teach us how to read and think about the Scriptures, so that "today" we will "hear his voice" (Psalm 95:7, 8), responding to God's word with faith, repentance, and obedience. As one of the official homilies of the Anglican tradition says, "Let us night and day muse and have

40

meditation and contemplation in them. Let us ruminate and as it were chew the cud, that we may have the sweet juice, spiritual effect, marrow, honey, kernel, taste, comfort and consolation of them."[10]

After each lesson is a *canticle*, pronounced *KAN-ti-kuhl*. The word means "song." The canticles teach us how to read the Scriptures—not as isolated bits, but as a coherent whole, seeing each passage as part of the revelation of God's plan of redemption. They teach us to respond to the Scriptures with gratitude and faith.[11]

For each canticle, you have two choices. Having choices is actually rare in the 1662 Book of Common Prayer—later prayer books have a huge number of choices, making them more complicated to use. It's easier to learn the 1662 versions of Morning and Evening Prayer, because pretty much the only choices you make are about the sentences and the canticles. But keep it simple. If you're just getting started with these services, when you come to a canticle, choose the first option. Both options serve the same function in the service.

At Morning Prayer, the first choice for the first canticle is the *Te Deum laudamus*, usually called simply the *Te Deum*, pronounced *tee DEE-uhm* or *tay DAY-uhm* (p. 6). The Latin name for each canticle comes from its opening word or words. In this hymn of praise, used in Christian worship since the 300s, we join our voices with those of the angels, the martyrs, and the church throughout the world. Together we offer praise and thanksgiving for the Triune God's work of creation and redemption.

The alternative on page 8 is the *Benedicite*, pronounced *ben-eh-DIE-see-tee*. This pre-Christian hymn of praise comes from the Greek version of the Book of Daniel, where it is sung by the three young men in the fiery furnace. These three young men are usually called by their Babylonian names, Shadrach, Meshach, and Abednego, but in the *Benedicite* they are called by their Hebrew names, Ananias, Azarias, and Misael. In this canticle, as in its likely model of Psalms 148–150, we praise God as Lord of all creation in heaven and earth, land and sea. The old custom is to say the *Benedicite* in Advent and Lent, and it gives to Morning Prayer a regular emphasis on the splendidness of the created world, and thus on the glory and goodness of its Maker.

The first choices for all the remaining canticles are from the Gospel of Luke. For the second canticle at Morning Prayer, the first choice is Zechariah's song (Luke 1:68-79). It is called the *Benedictus*, pronounced *ben-eh-DIK-tus*. At Evening Prayer the first choices for the canticles are the song of the Virgin Mary (Luke 1:46-55) and the song of Simeon (Luke 2:29-32). Mary's song is known as the *Magnificat*, pronounced *mag-NIF-i-kat*; and Simeon's song is called the *Nunc dimittis*, pronounced *nunk di-MI-tis*. These three canticles—the songs of Zechariah, the Virgin Mary, and Simeon—are called the Gospel Canticles. They encourage us to read the New Testament as the fulfillment of the promises made long ago to Abraham, David, and the prophets. The Gospel Canticles give Morning and Evening Prayer a Christological center.

After two lessons and two canticles comes the creed, or statement of belief. The word *creed* comes from the Latin *credo*, "I believe." Three creeds of the church are printed in the Book of Common Prayer: the Apostles' Creed, the Athanasian Creed, and the Nicene Creed. The Apostles' Creed is usually said at Morning and Evening Prayer (pp. 12, 22). It wasn't actually written by the apostles, but mostly consists of quotations or paraphrases from the apostolic writings. A recognizable form of the Apostles' Creed was used as early as the 300s, and by the 700s it reached its current form.

In saying the Apostles' Creed, you are expressing your own individual faith: "I believe." Yet it is not only your individual faith. In using the words of this ancient creed, you are joining with the other Christians gathered with you, expressing together the faith of the universal church. When we say these creeds, we are renewing our pledge of loyalty to God in the "company of all faithful people" (p. 265). That faith is not just intellectual assent (James 2:19), but an expression of our trust and confidence in Jesus Christ for salvation.

The creed's placement is important. It is first of all a response to hearing the Scriptures. Faith comes by hearing (Romans 10:17). Thomas Comber, who wrote an early commentary on the Book of Common Prayer, put it this way. "When we have heard [the word of God], it is fit we should profess our belief in it."[12] Yet the creed also looks forward to what comes next in the service. Comber goes on: "What follows the creed is the prayers, which are grounded on it. 'Faith is the fountain of prayers,' says St. Augustine; which is why the apostle says, 'How shall they call on him in whom they have not believed.' Therefore so we may pray, let us first believe."

4. *Praying*

Now we're ready for the last part of Morning and Evening Prayer: prayer. It's often been said that for a Christian, prayer is like breathing. The analogy works because it's something natural and instinctive. It happens all the time, and it's essential to life. But breathing happens without thinking about it. There are threats to breathing—like falling off a ship into the ocean—but we don't have to worry that we're going to get sidetracked and forget to breathe. But we *do* have to worry about distractions from prayer.

There are many ways prayer can "go wrong." We can lose our train of thought (compare the prayer on p. 700). We can be imbalanced, concentrating on just one need, or only on our own needs, or only on *needs*—there are many elements of prayer, not only petitions but also praise and thanksgiving. We can pray for things it would be better for us not to have. We can have a distorted view of God.

The prayers of the Book of Common Prayer are an antidote to each of these infections. They offer us a path of prayer, already laid out, to help us avoid distraction. They help us see clearly God's power, wisdom, and goodness. They offer a balance of different kinds of prayer, different kinds of petitions, and prayer for ourselves and others. As the exhortation at the beginning of Morning and Evening Prayer puts it, we "ask those things which are requisite and necessary, as well for the body as the soul."

44

At the start of these prayers there is a brief call and response. The leader says, "The Lord be with you," and the participants respond, "And with thy spirit" (pp. 12, 23). That's an ancient Christian greeting, drawing on different Scriptures, including Ruth 2:4 and 2 Timothy 4:22. Then the minister says, "Let us pray." This back-and-forth might seem a bit awkward when you first experience it, maybe even pointless, but it isn't. The spiritual point is that to pray as we should, we need God's presence. We've just confessed our faith by saying the creed, and now, united in this faith, we declare our charity for one another, our desire that the others we are praying with will also be blessed with God's presence. Here "charity" means the love we have for each other, the active love that desires the best for our fellow human beings. The best we can desire for others is God's own self, his presence with them. That charity will continue with the prayers for each other that follow.

More practically, the back-and-forth works against the constant pull of distractions. It keeps our minds from wandering. It centers us on the serious task at hand. Anyone who has ever had difficulty getting a crowd to stop talking and focus on saying grace before supper will understand the usefulness of this exchange.

Next follow five short sets of prayers, in increasing length. First, there are three lines that begin "Lord, have mercy upon us" (pp. 12, 23). This prayer is sometimes called by its Greek title, *Kyrie eleison*, pronounced *KI-ree-ay i-LAY-i-zon*. It's been used in Christian worship for at least sixteen hundred years, and it paraphrases a line in a parable told by Jesus: these are the words of the tax collector who knew he was a sinner and went home forgiven, not the words of the self-righteous Pharisee (Luke 18:9-14). On our lips, these words are a reminder of our need for divine mercy that we do not deserve—as we admitted earlier in the service in the general confession, "there is no health in us." The italicized line is a response. If you're reading the service with a group, the leader says "Lord, have mercy upon us," the other participants respond, and the leader repeats the first line.

Second, there is the Lord's Prayer (pp. 13, 23). We can approach God in prayer as "our Father" because we pray in his Son's name and by his Spirit (compare Galatians 4:6); we pray as those who are seeking his glory and dependent on his grace. When the Lord's Prayer was said the first time in the service, it was the pivot between forgiveness and praise, and it had the long ending of praise: "For thine is the kingdom, etc." Here the shorter form is used, and because it's at the start of our petitions, the emphasis falls on lines like "Give us this day our daily bread" and "deliver us from evil." We ask for what we need, knowing that God has already forgiven our sins and granted us what we need most of all: himself.

Third, there is a set of short petitions (pp. 13, 23). There are twelve lines, each a little prayer. They're organized into six pairs, and each pair is said responsively. These prayers are beautifully compact and weighty. They condense a huge number of prayers we could offer for salvation (pairs 1 and 4), external peace and security (pairs 2 and 5), and internal cleansing and righteousness (pairs 3 and 6). Most of these petitions are from the Psalms, but some are from other Scriptures. The notes sounded—salvation and peace, blessing on church and state—echo through the rest of the service.

Fourth, there are the "collects" (pp. 13, 24). Collect is pronounced *KAHL-ekt*, not *kuh-LEKT*. Developed in the ancient Latin-speaking church, a collect is a kind of short prayer that allows worshippers "to collect themselves and their thoughts in addressing God."[13] A collect usually asks for one thing and follows a certain structure.

Consider the collect for the Fourth Sunday after Trinity (p. 168). It begins by addressing God: "O God." Next it acknowledges a fact about God or ourselves that is the basis for the petition: "The protector of all who trust in thee, without whom nothing is strong, nothing is holy." Then comes the petition: "Increase and multiply upon us thy mercy." Notice the correspondence: we confidently ask God for mercy because he has revealed himself to be the protector of all who trust in him. After the petition is the aspiration, which is the purpose of the petition or its desired result: "That, thou being our ruler and guide, we may so pass through things temporal, that we finally lose not the things eternal." Last of all comes the pleading of Jesus Christ's name and merits. Often this is as short as "through Jesus Christ our Lord," but in the collect for the Fourth Sunday after Trinity it is its own sentence: "Grant this, O heavenly Father, for Jesus Christ's sake, our Lord. *Amen.*"

This is the typical structure of a collect: address, acknowledgment, petition, aspiration, pleading. Not all collects will have all five parts. Sometimes the pleading concludes with a doxology, such as "to whom, with thee and the Holy Ghost, be honour and glory, world without end" (as for example, in the collect for Advent 4 on p. 55). The collects are spiritual gems. They contain "a wealth of theology, and of ardent desire," and have a remarkable "ability to say so much in a few words."[14]

There are three collects in Morning Prayer and three in Evening Prayer. In both, the first is the "collect of the day." The collect of the day changes from week to week, and it's the main way we stay in step with the church year. The usual pattern is that each Sunday there is a new collect of the day, which is then used throughout the following week. For example, on Trinity Sunday and the following week, the collect of the day is the one on page 160. The next week, the collect of the day is the one for the First Sunday after Trinity (p. 162). (A number of the collects of the day will be discussed in chapters eight and nine.)

That leaves the second and third collects, which don't change from week to week, but they are different at Morning and Evening Prayer. These are old Latin prayers for peace and grace, going back to at least the 600s, and they were translated into English at the time of the Reformation by Archbishop Cranmer. One theme of these collects is divine protection—both gratitude for how God has protected us so far, and prayers that he would defend us from every enemy and danger we might encounter in the day or the night. In Morning Prayer, we begin with external threats (in the second collect) and then move to internal threats (in the third collect). In Evening Prayer the pattern is the reverse, beginning with internal threats and ending with a plea that God would protect us "from all perils and dangers of this night." These collects describe the God to whom our prayers are offered: God is the author of peace; he is the lover of concord; if we know him, we have eternal life; if we serve him, we have perfect freedom. And all those descriptions are in just one collect!

After the collects, there is a place to sing what the rubric calls an "anthem." (*Anthem* is in the glossary in the 1662 International Edition on p. 747.) If you're saying Morning or Evening Prayer with other people, this would be a place to sing a hymn. But you can also end the service with the third collect, skipping the anthem and everything after it.

The final set of prayers begins on page 14 for Morning Prayer and page 25 for Evening Prayer. These prayers begin by following the biblical instruction to pray for rulers (1 Timothy 2:1-2). In the 1662 Book of Common Prayer this is the place for the Prayer for the King's Majesty and the Prayer for the Royal Family. In the 1662 International Edition, these are replaced with two options for a Prayer for All Those in Civil Authority, and both options are suitable for any form of government. The first option is a prayer originally written by Archbishop Cranmer and adapted in the first prayer book of the Protestant Episcopal Church in the United States of America; the second is from a prayer book of the Anglican Church of Ghana.

Next is a prayer for the clergy and people. This is a translation by Archbishop Cranmer of a very old Latin prayer, and it asks that the Holy Spirit be sent down upon all churches, upon both the pastor of each church and the people. This prayer reminds us how far we've come on the journey through Morning or Evening Prayer. When we started, we said a prayer of confession that included "and there is no *health* in us." Now—forgiven, instructed by the Scriptures, approaching God in prayer—we ask God for the gift of "the *healthful* Spirit of thy grace," so we will be ready for service.

The next prayer, which the Book of Common Prayer calls "A Prayer of Saint Chrysostom," is from an ancient Greek liturgy. This prayer draws together all our other requests, asking God to grant them but only if they are for our good. It doesn't end with the usual "through Jesus Christ our Lord," because this prayer is actually to Christ himself: it is addressed to "Almighty God, who . . . dost promise that when two or three are gathered together in thy name" (Matthew 18:20).

The last prayer is a verse of Scripture, 2 Corinthians 13:14. It is called "the grace," because that is how it begins: "The grace of our Lord Jesus Christ, and the love of God, and the fellowship of the Holy Ghost, be with us all evermore." The people have the last word: "*Amen.*"

In Morning and Evening Prayer we follow a path of devotion that has been taken by countless Christians before you, and it will be taken by countless more in the generations to come. This path begins with honest confession. It ends with grace abounding.

AT A GLANCE: MORNING AND EVENING PRAYER

Preparing   Sentences of Scripture
                   Exhortation
                   Confession
                   Absolution
                   Lord's Prayer
                   Short prayers
                   Psalm 95 (Morning)

Praising   Psalms

Hearing   First lesson
                   First canticle
                   Second lesson
                   Second canticle
                   Creed

Praying   Greeting
                   Kyrie eleison
                   Lord's Prayer
                   Short prayers
                   Collects
                   Final prayers

4

Further Up and Further In

✠

DON'T READ THIS CHAPTER—at least not yet. It can take a while to get used to Morning and Evening Prayer, and you do want to get used to them. Let the novelty wear off, and let yourself settle into a habit of prayer and Bible reading.

But once you feel comfortable with Morning and Evening Prayer, you're ready for this chapter. It's about three ways to extend Morning and Evening Prayer, like an expansion pack for your daily prayers.

THE ATHANASIAN CREED

The first section after Evening Prayer starts on page 27 and seems to have a rather odd title: "At Morning Prayer." That's not really a title, as much as an indication of when it's used. Its actual title is "The Creed of St. Athanasius," and it's also known by its first words in Latin, *Quicunque vult*, pronounced *kwee-KOON-kweh voolt*. The Athanasian Creed is a detailed and careful statement of two doctrines that are central to the Christian faith. One is the Trinity: the doctrine that God is one substance and three persons. The other is the incarnation: the doctrine that the Son of God became man, taking a human body and human nature, and so is fully God and fully man. Perhaps it's a coincidence, but these two doctrines are also the ones that the church year is organized around. Half the church year, beginning with Advent, is dedicated to the feasts of the incarnation, while the other half is the season of Trinity. (These seasons are discussed in chapter eight.)

The background to this creed is a time when the church was ravaged by heresies, including the teachings of Arius, who denied that Jesus was truly and eternally God. Arius had many supporters, and at one point most of the church in the West actually supported him. But there were faithful bishops who taught the doctrine of the Trinity—and one was Saint Athanasius, the bishop of Alexandria during the mid-300s. Athanasius was a theological brawler and an ardent foe of heretics, especially of Arians and any others who denied the full deity of the Son of God. These controversies were settled by the Council of Nicaea (AD 325) and the Council of Constantinople (AD 381), both held under the watchful eye of the emperor. In settling these disputes, the church was forced to articulate systematically what the Scriptures teach about Jesus and his relationship to the Father and the

Holy Spirit. The church did this most famously in the Nicene Creed (p. 246).

The Athanasian Creed has been accepted in the Western Church as a statement of the orthodox teaching about the Trinity, spelling out details of the biblical teaching on the Trinity that are not addressed in the Nicene Creed, particularly the teachings of the Council of Chalcedon (AD 451) on Christ's human and divine natures. Despite the name, the Athanasian Creed wasn't actually written by Athanasius. It's associated with him because of his stalwart defense of the Trinity, but it probably dates to the 500s and seems to have been written in Gaul (modern-day France).

Sometimes objections to the Athanasian Creed are raised. One is that it speaks of the "catholic faith" (p. 27). But as in the other creeds, *catholic* means the universal church, not just the Roman Catholic Church.

Another objection is that this creed ties one's eternal fate to the presence or absence of good works (p. 30). But those lines, like so many in the creeds, are taken directly from the Bible (Matthew 25:31-46; John 5:28-29). These good works are not the reason we are justified, that is, counted righteous by God. Instead, as one of the Articles puts it, good works are "pleasing and acceptable to God in Christ, and do spring out necessarily of a true and lively faith; insomuch that by them a lively faith may be as evidently known as a tree discerned by the fruit" (Article 12, p. 632; also "A Sermon of the Salvation of Mankind," pp. 654-69).

Still another objection is to the opening sentences of the creed, which say that to be saved one must "hold" and "keep" the catholic faith. To be sure, a person doesn't have to know all the technicalities of the Athanasian Creed in order to be saved—the thief on the cross did not have to memorize this creed before Jesus could say to him, "Today you will be with me in Paradise" (Luke 23:43 RSV). But the creed does state the catholic faith, based on the Scriptures (Article 8, p. 631), and it expresses in stern language the necessity of adhering to that faith (compare 2 Timothy 1:13-14). The Athanasian Creed reminds us of the importance of right belief as a basis for right action, and it is "a warning to those who hold the Catholic faith about the dangers of letting it go."[1]

The rubric before the Athanasian Creed lists the days on which it's said. On those feast days, when you say Morning Prayer and get to the Apostles' Creed on page 12, say the Athanasian Creed instead. The frequency works out to about once a month.

Litany

The prayers at the end of Morning and Evening Prayer encompass every kind of need. But those prayers are short and light on detail. If only there were a longer set of prayers that could be added on. There is!

The Litany starts on page 31. The rubric under the title calls it a form of "general supplication," the kind of prayer the apostle Paul urges us to offer in 1 Timothy 2:1-2. The Litany is the way Morning Prayer concludes on Sundays, Wednesdays, and Fridays. On these days, the Litany replaces the last four prayers—from the Prayer for All Those in Civil Authority on page 14 through the Grace on page 16. It can also be used as a standalone prayer service, and it can be expanded to address specific needs and occasions (drawing on the "Prayers and Thanksgivings" section right after it). The choice of these three days of the week for the Litany isn't random. It reflects how Christians as early as the 100s distinguished these days because of events in the life of our Lord—feasting on Sundays to remember his resurrection, fasting on Fridays to remember his death, and in some places fasting on Wednesdays to remember his betrayal in Gethsemane.

The Litany was the first English liturgy authorized by the Church of England—in 1544, five years before the rest of the Book of Common Prayer. Archbishop Cranmer started with the medieval Latin litany of the saints, but he also drew from Martin Luther's prior adaptation of the Roman litany, William Marshall's prior English version of Luther, and the liturgy of Saint Chrysostom. With all of these rich threads woven together, and a little more tinkering along the way, the Litany is "a common treasure house of all good devotion."[2]

The Litany begins with a solemn invocation of the Trinity. Next is a series of short prayers for deliverance from evils of body and soul, an expansion of "deliver us from evil" in the Lord's Prayer. These short prayers are traditionally called the "deprecations" (from the Latin *deprecari*, a prayer to ward off evil).

Then follow the key events of Christ's ministry, which we plead as the basis for our deliverance. These prayers, traditionally called the "obsecrations" (from the Latin *obsecrare*, meaning "to beg for the sake of something sacred"), remind us that Christ alone is the ground of our hope.

Next are prayers not just for ourselves but for the whole church, for our country and its leaders, the clergy, all Christians, and those in special need. We also ask that we would have the graces needed for faith and a holy life. These prayers, the "intercessions," conclude with the Lord's Prayer—as always, a reminder that we come to the Father as disciples of his Son—and a final set of "supplications," in which the urgency of our need is pressed home. Then the Litany concludes with the same two prayers that conclude Morning and Evening Prayer: the Prayer of Saint Chrysostom and the Grace.

J. I. Packer called the Litany "a ten-minute prayer service" that "stands as a pattern of prayer for all time." Packer said that the Litany "drills us in the art of conversation with God in three ways."

First, "it teaches us to know ourselves as sinners. The Litany has a majestic view of God as sovereign and just, and hence takes a humbling view of man as weak and sinful."

Second, "it teaches us to know God as our Saviour. Through Jesus' mediation and the coming of the Holy Ghost, God pardons, protects, and empowers for holy living. Man's need is great, but God can meet it. That is the gospel of the Litany."

Third, "it teaches us to know others as our neighbours. Knowing God's love to us, we love him in return, and when we love God every man becomes our neighbour, to be loved for his sake. So the Litany leads us on from personal trust in Christ to pray that God will have mercy on all men."[3]

OCCASIONAL PRAYERS AND THANKSGIVINGS

The last part of the expansion pack for the daily offices is a set of prayers for certain public occasions. These are events affecting an entire society—like drought, famine, war, and plague.

After six of these prayers are ones for the "Ember Weeks" (p. 41). These are four weeks that are evenly spaced through the year: one each in spring, summer, fall, and winter. In these four weeks, the Wednesday, Friday, and Saturday are called "Ember Days" (p. xxv). No one knows for sure where the word *ember* comes from, but the most likely explanation is that it's from an Old English word for a period of time, especially thought of as a round or cycle of time (*ymbryne*). With this quarterly cycle of Ember Days, "adrift among various occupations, cares, the frailties of life—and with God's grace—the Church halts the flow of time and reflects in a religious way upon all that happens with and to us."[4] The Ember Days can be traced back to the 400s in Rome, and they are especially a time to fast and pray for those being ordained as ministers.[5]

Next is a prayer that is much loved by users of the Book of Common Prayer, the Prayer for All Conditions of Men (p. 43), that is, for all different kinds of people and their needs. It prays for a variety of needs, including for the church's faithfulness and unity, and for everyone who is "afflicted or distressed, in mind, body, or estate." (*Estate* is in the glossary on p. 751.) This prayer includes a phrase that echoes through the work of tens of thousands of Anglican missionaries over the last four centuries: "thy saving health unto all nations."

Also much loved is the next prayer, the General Thanksgiving (p. 44). It helps us not overlook what God has done for us—"our creation, preservation, and all the blessings of this life"—and to see all these blessings in relation to God's greatest gift—"above all, for thine inestimable love in the redemption of the world by our Lord Jesus Christ."

You can pray the Prayer for All Conditions of Men and the General Thanksgiving as written, or you can personalize them. They include places where you can add the names of people you are praying for and specific blessings you are thankful for.

There is a ready-made spot for these occasional prayers and thanksgivings in Morning and Evening Prayer. Under the title of this section is the line "to be used before the two final prayers of the Litany or of Morning and Evening Prayer" (p. 39). That means you can insert any of these prayers and thanksgivings right before the Prayer of Saint Chrysostom and the Grace—the last two prayers said in the Litany or in Morning or Evening Prayer.

This illustrates the simplicity and usability of the 1662 Book of Common Prayer. These prayers and thanksgivings aren't in the text of Morning and Evening Prayer, so someone who's just getting used to those services doesn't have to flip through them all. If you don't know about them, they are not in your way. But if you do know about them, you can insert them, and they offer wise words to carry you through times of great trial and great deliverance.

This section gives us words to pray in times of crisis. How these prayers talk about these times and about our leaders—especially about sickness, suffering, and war—may strike you as unusual, even jarring. This isn't the way most of us are used to talking about these things today. But the language of these prayers comes straight from the Bible, and it's closer to how Christians in the early centuries of the church talked and prayed about these things. Praying these prayers has the potential, as the apostle Paul puts it, to transform our minds (Romans 12:2).

Some of the occasions marked by these prayers might have seemed out of date a few years ago. In prayer books compiled in the late twentieth and early twenty-first centuries, there are no prayers for plague and war. Perhaps the idea was that we'd gotten past all that unpleasantness. Unfortunately, events in our world have made the wisdom of these prayers once again clear.

One last note. The occasional prayers and thanksgivings that begin on page 39 are all from the 1662 Book of Common Prayer. If you want still more, the 1662 International Edition includes an appendix with additional prayers and thanksgivings drawn from around the world (pp. 670-718).

5

The Ascent Continues: Baptism and Confirmation

✠

MORNING AND EVENING PRAYER are designed for a Christian community. They're meant for Christians—in a church, or even a school or home—to gather together to say these prayers and hear God's word. But they don't require any other people. You can read Morning or Evening Prayer by yourself. The sacraments of baptism and communion are different. In the Book of Common Prayer, these services do require other people. There are no solo sacraments: the place where the sacraments are "ministered according to Christ's ordinance" is the church, among God's people (Article 19, pp. 635-36).

Let's start with a definition. What exactly is a *sacrament*? Different churches use the word in different ways, but the catechism in the Book of Common Prayer defines a sacrament this way: "An outward and visible sign of an inward and spiritual grace, given unto us, ordained by Christ himself, as a means by which we receive that grace, and a pledge to assure us thereof" (p. 305). So a sacrament has two parts: something outward, the visible sign; and something inward, the spiritual grace. A sacrament is not a sign of a natural phenomenon, like smoke is a sign of fire. Instead, it is a sign given by God. And a sacrament isn't something added later by the apostles or the church—it was ordained by Jesus Christ.

To say that a sacrament is a sign means that it points to something else (the spiritual grace). But the sacraments are more than mere signs. If they are received in faith, they aren't just pointers, but are means that God uses to bring about and strengthen his work in us. In other words, they *point to and convey* a spiritual grace. A sacrament is both a "means" that God uses to give us that spiritual grace and also a "pledge" that gives us confidence that God has given us this grace. As the Communion service puts it, in words over-flowing with comfort, the sacraments "assure us" of God's "favour and goodness towards us" (p. 265).

For one sacrament the outward sign is water, and for the other, bread and wine. What are the spiritual realities that each sacrament communicates to those who receive them with faith? For baptism, these spiritual realities are death to sin and new birth as a child of God (p. 305). For the Lord's Supper, they are eating Christ's body and blood, the very food of the soul, and an entwining of our souls with God, as Christ dwells in us and we dwell in him (p. 306). The sacraments are divinely established means by which we share in the life of God in Christ.

This chapter is a guide to the service of Holy Baptism, and chapter six to the service of Holy Communion. This chapter also considers what's supposed to happen in between the two sacraments: instruction and confirmation in the faith. For more about the sacraments in general, read the catechism (pp. 300, 304-6), the Articles of Religion (pp. 637-45), and the homily from the Second Book of Homilies called "Of Common Prayer and Sacraments."[1]

BAPTISM

When you walk into an old English church, often the first thing you come to is a stone baptismal font, set in the nave, near the entrance. There is symbolism to that placement: baptism is the entrance to the church, the beginning of the Christian life. And this is how the gospels all begin: John the Baptist is calling God's people to repent and be baptized. Throughout the New Testament, baptism is associated with death and birth, death to one kind of life and new birth to another (Romans 6:1-11). Out with being a sinful child of Adam and in with being a forgiven child of God. That is why it makes sense to think about the sacrament of baptism first.

The Book of Common Prayer has not one but three baptismal services! The first is for infants and small children when the baptism happens in church (p. 271). The second is for private use when the infant is gravely ill, maybe even at the point of death, and there is no time to wait for a baptism in church (p. 281). The third is for the baptism of those old enough to speak for themselves, which would include adolescents and adults (p. 289). All three services express the same teaching about baptism but adapt it to different circumstances.

We'll walk through the baptism service for infants in church, because it's the most widely used. Infant baptism is approved by the prayer book, not only in the services for infant baptism but also in the catechism (p. 305); and the Articles of Religion call it "most agreeable with the institution of Christ" (Article 27, p. 639). But neither the Book of Common Prayer nor the Articles give a historical defense, so for that we will need to look elsewhere.[2] But what the prayer book does do is closely tie baptism and its benefits to personal faith. Look for this connection as we go through the service, especially if you have concerns that infant baptism could sideline faith.

The Public Baptism of Infants service is not read by itself, but is inserted into Morning or Evening Prayer immediately after the second lesson, which is from the New Testament (p. 271). That means the sequence is New Testament lesson, then baptism, then the second canticle and Apostles' Creed. This placement means that the baptism both illustrates the good news of the gospel (the New Testament lesson just read), and is also part of the response to hearing the good news (with the canticle and creed). And so, in a stroke of liturgical genius, immediately after the baptism, the congregation sings the *Benedictus* (p. 11) or *Nunc dimittis* (p. 22)—two songs that were occasioned by the birth of a child and that revel in the fulfillment of God's promises. Truly, "mine eyes have seen thy salvation" (p. 22).

The main elements of the service are prayers, vows, and signs. The service begins with prayers and vows. At the very start is the soaring Flood Prayer, which ties baptism into the great events of salvation through water in the Old Testament and the baptism of Jesus in the New (bottom of p. 272). Before the Flood Prayer appeared in the Book of Common Prayer, it was used in the earliest German liturgies from the Reformation churches of Wittenberg and Zurich. The italics show which words will need to be altered based on the sex or the number of the people being baptized. The vows are made by the godparents (pp. 275-76). The godparents have a very important role in the service (but more on that in a moment). There is also a reading from the Gospel of Mark, which connects the baptism of infants with Jesus blessing the children and taking them into his arms, just like the priest will do in baptism.

Next comes the key moment—the sign of baptism. The priest takes the child into his hands, asks the name of the child, and then baptizes the child, saying, "[Name], I baptize thee in the name of the Father, and of the Son, and of the Holy Ghost" (pp. 277-78). That action exactly follows the command of our Lord in Matthew 28:19. The naming underscores that the child's identity is in Christ.

Immediately after the baptism, the priest makes the sign of the cross on the forehead of the newly baptized child. During the first century of the prayer book's use, the sign of the cross in baptism was deeply controversial, and some

Puritan critics objected to a ceremony that was not prescribed by Scripture. But the prayer book pushes back. It cites a church law, or "canon," that defends the sign of the cross in baptism (p. 280).[3] And the baptism service explains what the sign of the cross in baptism means: it is a token, or symbol, that through the sacrament this person has joined the company of those who are not ashamed to confess Christ and will fight under his banner (p. 278). In baptism we are enrolled in the church militant. The sign of the cross—this symbol of Christ's extreme suffering for us, but also of his victory over sin and death—is a graphic reminder that as Christians we are engaged in a lifelong battle against the world, the flesh, and the devil (Ephesians 6:10-20; pp. 32, 300). This is the only time the Book of Common Prayer has the sign of the cross. This use and explanation fit a larger pattern in the prayer book: there is a sparing use of ceremonies, they are simple, they are ancient, and their significance is explained, all with the goal of edifying the people (see pp. xvii-xxi).

Next comes the Lord's Prayer, and its placement here is not an accident. In the Book of Common Prayer, there are two patterns for saying the Lord's Prayer. Sometimes it appears at the beginning of a service as preparation. Other times it appears right after the high point of a service.[4] That second pattern is why the Lord's Prayer is said after the response to the word of God in Morning and Evening Prayer, after partaking of the body and blood of Christ in Holy Communion, and here after the baptism of the child. The Lord's Prayer has a particular resonance in this service, as baptism into Christ Jesus gives us the right to address God as "Our Father" (Galatians 3:26-27).

Next comes another prayer, a thanksgiving (p. 279). It is made up of many biblical phrases, and it thanks God for answering the prayers made before the baptism.

Finally, there is the exhortation to the godparents (pp. 279-80), mirroring the vows made by the godparents at the start of the service. Godparents have an important role in baptism. To understand why, we have to see the importance of faith in the baptismal services of the Book of Common Prayer. And to understand this, it will help to see how the prayer book charts a different course on baptism than some other Christian traditions.

In the Scriptures, baptism is strongly associated with repentance (Matthew 3:11; Acts 2:38). That is, baptism represents both a turning *from* and a turning *to*; both a renouncing of the world, the flesh, and the devil, and a following of God and his commandments. It is a death and a new birth (Romans 6:4). Some churches teach that you're supposed to have faith first, and afterward you are baptized, as a testimony to your belief. This is a widely held view among Baptists, for example. Yet the New Testament strongly associates baptism with new birth, or *regeneration*, a word that in the Bible means "new birth" (John 3:5; Titus 3:5). And the New Testament describes the benefit of baptism in several different ways—the forgiveness of sins (Acts 22:16), the coming of the Holy Spirit (Acts 2:38), being united to Christ (Romans 6:3-4), and being received into the church (Acts 2:41). It is not just a testimony.

Other churches will say that baptism confers this benefit automatically, "by the very fact of the action's being performed."[5] Yet just as many Scriptures say we are united to Christ in baptism, there are also many Scriptures that say we are united to Christ by personal faith, and not simply the faith of the church (Ephesians 2:8-9). Sometimes these Scriptures are right next to each other (Galatians 3:26-27; Colossians 2:12)!

How can we hold all this together? The answer in the Book of Common Prayer is that baptism is a sign—a pointer to a spiritual reality—but not a mere sign. The sacraments are "effectual signs of grace and God's good will towards us, by the which he doth work invisibly in us" (Article 25, pp. 637-38). Through baptism God can apply the forgiveness of sins, empower us with the Holy Spirit, unite us to Christ, and welcome us into the church. In fact, that is exactly what we pray for at the start of the baptismal service (pp. 272-3). As the Apostles' Creed says, there is "one baptism for the remission"—which means cancellation—"of sin" (p. 22). But this benefit is assured only for those who "receive baptism rightly" (Article 27, p. 639). The way to rightly receive this sacrament is to repent and believe (p. 305). So receiving baptism in faith is absolutely critical, and the service emphasizes this on nearly every page.

That's where the godparents come in. An adult who is being baptized has to promise to renounce the devil, to follow Christ, and to live a life of faith and repentance. But what about an infant? Even though baptism may be described as laying the foundation of faith, and sowing a seed that will later ripen,[6] the infant still cannot make these promises. But these promises are so important to the service of baptism that *someone* has to make them for the child. The logic of godparents is that they stand in for the child; they are trusted adults who make these promises on the child's behalf. If the baptized child is like an infant who inherits a great estate, the godparents are like the trustees who care for the estate until the child reaches maturity.

So the godparents are the way the baptismal service holds together three things: the efficacy of baptism (as a means of grace, not merely a sign pointing to grace); infant baptism, the ancient and once universal practice of the Christian church, strongly embraced by the Protestant reformers; and the necessity of faith in Jesus Christ. The gifts of baptism are not for one moment only, but for our entire lives.[7] Yet even though the gifts of baptism must be received in time, the Christian child is treated in the meantime as exactly that— not as a young unbeliever who might someday grow up and come to faith, but as already a new Christian, a person just learning to walk as a Christian, like the children the apostles Paul and John wrote to in the first century (Ephesians 6:1; Colossians 3:20; 1 John 2:12).

Eventually, the child does have to take on himself or herself these promises, publicly committing to follow Jesus Christ. That is done in the rite of confirmation, after the child is taught the Christian faith. (That service is discussed in the next part of this chapter.) For now, the godparents make these promises on the child's behalf, and they commit themselves to ensure that the child is taught and instructed in the Christian faith. Among other things, the godparents are responsible for making sure the child hears sermons and memorizes the Apostles' Creed, the Lord's Prayer, and the Ten Commandments (pp. 287-88). This is why even adults who are baptized still have godparents—even though the godparents don't make the promises, they are mature Christians who offer guidance and support.

If you aren't used to baptismal services from the Book of Common Prayer, there will be some surprises. There are several prayers for what God will do in baptism, the sign of the cross, lots of emphasis on instruction, and probably most surprising of all, godparents. But if you give it a chance, you will find yourself amazed by the service's power and beauty. The whole congregation joins together in prayer, confidently trusting in God's work, witnessing the solemn vows of the godparents, and seeing this day as one more chapter in the long story of God's deliverance of his people through water—from Noah's ark and the crossing of the Red Sea, to Jesus' baptism and the baptism of this child today.

Between the Sacraments: The Christian ABCs

Baptism is the sacrament that begins our life as children of God. Communion is the sacrament that sustains our life—of Christ dwelling in us and us dwelling in him. Baptism has to come first: we have to start our life in Christ before we can continue our life in Christ. But once we're baptized, does anything need to happen before we receive communion?

In the Book of Common Prayer, the answer is yes. Before receiving the sacrament of communion, a person needs to be instructed in the faith. The apostle Paul warned the Christians in Corinth that before they took the sacrament of the body and blood of the Lord, they needed to examine themselves, so they did not receive the sacrament "unworthily" (1 Corinthians 11:27-29). In the Book of Common Prayer, this biblical idea of approaching Communion the right way—with repentance and faith—is illustrated by the Communion exhortations (pp. 251-6). Those exhortations are directed to people who already have basic training in the Christian faith.

When those baptized as infants come to an age where they are able to, they should publicly take responsibility for the vows made on their behalf in baptism. But they can only do that if they are first instructed in what those vows mean. James Ussher, a learned theologian and Archbishop of Armagh in Ireland (1625–1656), once wrote, "All the promises of grace were in my baptism given to me as an estate, and sealed to me on God's part, but then I come to have their profit and benefit when I come to understand the gift that God has sealed to me in baptism, and actually lay hold of it by faith."[8]

To examine ourselves, in order to rightly receive the sacrament of communion, we don't have to be perfect Christians. No one is! But we do need to know the basics of the Christian faith. These two important things—being instructed in the Christian ABCs, and making a public profession of our faith— are brought together in the catechism and confirmation.

In the century and a half after the Reformation began, many of the Protestant churches developed catechisms to equip the baptized for their new life in Christ. These included Martin Luther's catechisms; the Heidelberg and Westminster catechisms; and the catechisms written by Alexander Nowell, who was dean of St. Paul's from 1561 to 1602.[9] The prayer book catechism has much in common with those catechisms, but it is brief. In just seven pages it offers an overview of the Christian faith.

The prayer book catechism starts precisely where the service for the Public Baptism of Infants leaves off, by asking the child what was done by the godparents (p. 300). The vows taken on the child's behalf included the rejection of the world, the flesh, and the devil, and this rejection made the baptized person a target of assault by this infernal triad. With the signing of the cross in baptism, the baptized person was marked as a Christian soldier. Now the catechism is meant to arm that soldier for battle, and it does this with instruction in the Apostles' Creed, Ten Commandments, and Lord's Prayer.

Each subject is taught in a Q and A format. The emphasis is not only on reciting these texts—which are regularly used in the Book of Common Prayer liturgies—but also on understanding them. A child or adult learning the catechism will develop a basic sense of what a Christian believes, does, and prays. The final section on the sacraments ends with the self-examination necessary for coming to the Lord's table. Thus the catechism forms a bridge between baptism and communion.

Instruction in the catechism is supposed to culminate in "The Order of Confirmation" (p. 308). The catechism and confirmation are so closely tied together that they're a single line in the table of contents. But what is confirmation?

Confirmation is a very old rite, going back to the first millennium of the church. What the Church of England did with it at the Reformation is typical of the Book of Common Prayer: keep the rite, but simplify it, pruning away ceremonies that had built up around the service and bringing a new Reformation emphasis on faith through hearing God's word.

In the Book of Common Prayer, confirmation has four purposes:

1. It ensures that those who are baptized receive instruction in the basics of the Christian faith. This instruction is necessary for participation in the Lord's Supper.

2. It provides a public ceremony for individuals to personally ratify the faith into which they were baptized. In different churches confirmation happens at different ages, such as 7 to 12, though it depends on the child.

3. It includes a prayer for daily strengthening in the Holy Spirit, who was given in baptism.

4. Because confirmation is administered by the bishop, when those who are being confirmed make their profession of faith, it is witnessed not just by the local congregation but by the broader church. That's because the bishop is the representative of the catholic

church (in the sense of the universal church); in his person the catholicity and antiquity of the church are visible.

These purposes are all clear in the service itself. A person who wants to be confirmed has to be instructed in the catechism (pp. 280, 307, 308). As the service begins, the person being confirmed makes a public profession of faith. Then the bishop prays that the gifts of God's grace would "daily increase" in those being confirmed. Laying hands on the head of each person being confirmed, the bishop offers a prayer and blessing.

The words of the bishop's blessing are a reminder that the Christian life isn't clear sailing. There are temptations to resist. There are foes to defeat. The bishop says: "Defend, O Lord, this thy child, with thy heavenly grace, that *he* may continue thine for ever, and daily increase in thy Holy Spirit more and more until *he* come unto thy everlasting kingdom. Amen" (p. 310).

The prayer book catechism and confirmation service aren't the end of the road for someone's instruction in the Christian faith. They are meant to lay a good foundation. They're supposed to ensure, as the collect for Saint Mark's Day puts it, that Christians are "established in the truth" of the "holy gospel" (p. 217).

6

Ascending to Heaven: Holy Communion

✝

WHEN JESUS SPOKE, his words summoned up pictures in the minds of everyone who heard him. Shepherds and sheep, vines and branches, the seed cast by the sower. One picture Jesus often evoked was a feast. When the prodigal son returns from the far country, the father is already running to meet him, and he hurries the son home to celebrate his return with a feast (Luke 15). Jesus told another parable about a wedding feast where those who were invited did not come, but room was made for others (Matthew 22:1-14).

The actions of Jesus also proclaimed a feast for the people of God. When Jesus fed the five thousand, the bread never ran out. This is the only one of Jesus' miracles that is recorded in all of the gospels. And three of the gospels describe the Last Supper as a Passover meal, the annual feast by which all Jews remembered and participated in the great act of divine deliverance, the Exodus (Matthew 26:19-29).

These pictures of a feast come together in Holy Communion. In this sacrament, the table is laid with bread and wine for those who have come home from the far country, for those who have been brought in from outside for the marriage supper, for those who are fed with lavish abundance, for those who are remembering and participating in the greatest of all acts of divine deliverance, the death of our crucified Savior.

Where does this feasting happen? One answer is that it happens right there in church, as you kneel near the communion table and eat the piece of bread handed to you and drink from the chalice. As one of the great Reformation catechisms puts it, "as surely as I receive from the hand of the one who serves, and taste with my mouth the bread and cup of the Lord, given me as sure signs of Christ's body and blood, so surely he nourishes and refreshes my soul for eternal life with his crucified body and poured-out blood."[1] And that is true.

But the Book of Common Prayer also suggests another, perhaps more surprising place where this feast is held. We are invited by Jesus, the Lord of the feast and the sacrificial Lamb, who "ascended into heaven, and sitteth on the right hand of the Father" (Nicene Creed, p. 246). But how can we attend a heavenly feast? John Jewel—one of the leaders of the English Reformation, exiled under Queen Mary and later made Bishop of Salisbury under Queen Elizabeth I— recognized that this was exactly the question: "The body then which we eat is in heaven: above all angels, and archangels, and powers, and principalities. Our food is in heaven on high, and we are here below on the earth. How can it be that we may reach it, or taste, or eat it?"[2] Watch how this question is answered in the Communion service.

This service has five parts:

- preparing
- hearing (the gospel read and preached)
- offering (both monetary offerings and prayers)
- communing
- thanksgiving

Some of these elements are also in Morning and Evening Prayer—those services, too, have preparing, hearing, and prayer. But in the Communion service there are new elements: a focus on the gospel and its proclamation in the sermon, the offering, and especially the communion and thanksgiving, as we receive the consecrated bread and wine and offer ourselves to God in gratitude.

Today the Communion service is often used by itself, but that's not how it's designed to be used. It's really intended to be part of a sequence: Morning Prayer, Litany, and Holy Communion, one right after another.

1. Preparing

Two common assumptions people have today are surprisingly new in Anglican worship: the assumption that communion will be offered every week, and the assumption that most people attending the service will receive communion.

Before the Reformation, the people were required to take communion once a year at Easter. The Book of Common Prayer increased the frequency, requiring that parishioners receive communion "at least three times in the year, of which Easter shall be one" (p. 269). Communion might be offered more frequently still, but only those who had intentionally prepared to receive it on a given occasion stayed for that part of the service. After Morning Prayer, the Litany, and the first part of the Communion service—through page 251—those who were not receiving communion would leave the church. A pattern of monthly or quarterly Communion services remained the usual practice in most Anglican churches until the second half of the twentieth century.

Why wouldn't everyone receive communion every week? Why might communion be offered, but a large part of the congregation not stay to receive it? To answer these questions, remember that the sacrament of Christ's body and blood is a feast, the greatest feast—and for a really important feast, we have to get ready. The preparation for receiving communion doesn't actually start in the service. It starts a week earlier when the minister announces the Communion service and reads one of the two exhortations on pages 251-55. Those exhortations are worth reading carefully, because they sum up what the Scriptures teach about how to approach the Lord's Supper, drawing especially on the instructions the apostle Paul gave to the Corinthian church (1 Corinthians 11:17-34).

Preparing to receive this sacrament is a theme in the prayer book. Morning and Evening Prayer prepare us as we acknowledge our sins, reaffirm our faith, and express our love for our neighbors through prayer. The rubrics at the start of the Communion service are a guide (pp. 241-2), and the Ten Commandments have traditionally been understood as a template for examining our own conduct to prepare to receive the sacrament (pp. 243-44). Many other parts of the book are also useful for this self-examination, including the Litany (p. 31), the Commination service (p. 353), the Psalms (p. 362), and the catechism (p. 306). And there are additional prayers specifically for preparing for Communion (pp. 694-99). The point of preparation is not to wallow in our failures; it is to honestly recognize our helplessness and need for the mercy offered by "the Lord, whose property is always to have mercy" (p. 261).

And now it's time. We're ready for the Communion service to start. The very first words we say are those of the Lord's Prayer (p. 242). Before the Reformation, this was said silently in Latin by the priest, after he put on his vestments and was preparing to offer the sacrifice of the Mass. The change in the Book of Common Prayer is intentional and dramatic: all the people say the Lord's Prayer because all the people together are preparing to offer to God their sacrifice of praise and thanksgiving. With this prayer we are asking God to orient our hearts toward his kingdom. We are also asking for sustaining bread—a prayer that will soon be answered.

Next comes an ancient Latin prayer that was translated into English at the Reformation (p. 242). It's usually called "The Collect for Purity," but it could just as easily be called

"The Collect of the Heart." It refers to hearts twice. First, God knows our hearts. Second, we ask that God would cleanse our hearts by "the inspiration of thy Holy Spirit." (*Inspiration* is in the glossary on page 753.) And why do we want God to purify our hearts? So we can do two things: "perfectly love" and "worthily magnify" God. In other words, love and worship.

Thinking about love and worship—about how our hearts should love God above all things and worship him alone—leads us directly into the Ten Commandments (p. 243). If that sounds surprising, remember how Jesus summed up the law: love the Lord with all your heart and love your neighbor as yourself (Matthew 22:37-40). The Ten Commandments tell us how to do that, with the first four commandments teaching us to love God and the last six teaching us to love our neighbor.

Each commandment is read by the minister, and after each one the congregation says (or sings) a response. For the first nine commandments, the response is "Lord, have mercy upon us, and incline our hearts to keep this law." After the last commandment, the response is "Lord, have mercy upon us, and write all these thy laws in our hearts, we beseech thee." That's ten more times we refer to our hearts, asking God to turn them and inscribe his law upon them. The last response echoes the words of the prophet Jeremiah, who foretold the new covenant: "I will put my law within them, and I will write it on their hearts; and I will be their God, and they shall be my people" (Jeremiah 31:33 NRSV; also Hebrews 10:16).

Next comes a collect for civil authorities (p. 245). To understand why, we need a bit of Reformation theology. The reformers taught that the law of God, especially as summarized in the Ten Commandments, had three uses.

First, there was the "civil" use. The Ten Commandments serve as a guide to rulers and can help restrain sinful acts that threaten the stability of society. It's not an accident, for example, that societies have property laws that prohibit theft. The precepts of the Ten Commandments are rooted in nature, in how God made human beings and how our societies operate.

Second, there's the "pedagogical" use. *Pedagogical* means teaching, and specifically it picks up on language from the apostle Paul about the law being a "schoolmaster" (*paidogogos*), also translated "tutor" or "guardian," to drive us onward to faith in Christ (Galatians 3:24). The idea is that we look at the law and see that we fall short. Knowing we cannot keep the law, knowing that we need someone else's perfect righteousness, we run to Jesus.

Third, there's the "moral" use. Here the idea is that for the Christian—the person justified through faith in Christ—the law is a guide for how to please God (Psalm 119). We are "saved by grace through faith," but are not then free to live however we want, for we are "his handiwork, made in Christ Jesus for the good works for which God readied us" (Ephesians 2:8, 10 Lattimore). How do we know what those good works are? Here the law comes to our aid, for it shows with vivid specificity what it means to love God and neighbor.

Now that we know about these three uses of the law, think back to the congregational response after each commandment. It starts with "Lord, have mercy upon us." That's the pedagogical use of the law—we know our sinfulness and our need of divine righteousness (Luke 18:13-14). And how does the congregational response continue? Asking God to "incline our hearts" and "write . . . in our hearts" these laws. That's the moral use of the law. So what's missing?

The only use of the law that we haven't had yet is the civil use. So now the Ten Commandments are followed with a prayer for rulers, asking God to govern their hearts (p. 245)—there is that word *hearts* again. And while restraining wickedness is not sufficient to save anyone, this use of the law is not divorced from the gospel. Restraining vice establishes a context in which the gospel can flourish. The apostle Paul told Timothy to lead the Ephesian church in praying "for kings, and for all that are in authority; that we may lead a quiet and peaceable life in all godliness and honesty" (1 Timothy 2:2 KJV, echoed in the Litany on p. 33).

Now we are ready for the last part of the preparation. This is the collect of the day (p. 246)—the prayer that keeps us in step with the church calendar. Because the collect of the day is also said in Morning and Evening Prayer, it binds those daily services to the Communion service.

2. Hearing

Once we are prepared, we hear two biblical readings. The first is called "the epistle," and is usually from one of the epistles. The second is called "the gospel," and is always from one of the four gospels. After the gospel, the congregation responds in faith with the words of the Nicene Creed. This might remind you of Morning and Evening Prayer. In those services there were two readings (the lessons) followed by a creed. Here there are two readings (epistle and gospel) followed by a creed. But there are important differences. At Morning and Evening Prayer, there is simply a lot more Scripture and a lot more response. Before the lessons there are psalms; the lessons themselves tend to be much longer (usually a chapter each); and after each lesson there is a canticle of response. Only after all that do we have the creed.

But in the Communion service the reading of the Scriptures is streamlined. The readings in Morning and Evening Prayer give us a broad familiarity with the entirety of Scripture, but the epistle and gospel readings are usually shorter and topically focused. This annual sequence of epistle and gospel readings is organized around the divine plan of redemption in Christ. In the Communion service, not only does the Nicene Creed teach us to respond to these readings, but it is also the doorway we pass through to the sacrament: only by faith can we partake of the body and blood of Christ.

There's also an important addition that is not part of the "script" of Morning and Evening Prayer—a sermon. There's a rubric in the Communion service saying there has to be a sermon (p. 247). So Morning and Evening Prayer immerse us in lots and lots of Scripture, as we read in order through the Psalms and most of the Old Testament, New Testament, and Apocrypha. But the Communion service pulls out key passages—almost always from the New Testament, and pairs two of these passages, which are the basis for a sermon about our salvation and life in Christ. (We'll go deeper into these different ways of reading the Scriptures in chapter seven.) The sermon could also be one of "the homilies set forth by authority," which are in the two official Books of Homilies. (Those are discussed in chapter ten.)

The prayer book makes the sermon a necessary component of the Communion because preaching is being viewed as a means of grace, as a divinely appointed method for implanting and stirring up faith within hearers (Romans 10:14). And hearing the sermon is part of the ascent. It points us to Jesus, the one to whom we are united by faith. Archbishop Cranmer put it this way: "For as the word of God preached puts Christ into our ears, so likewise these elements of water, bread, and wine—joined to God's word—after a sacramental manner put Christ into our eyes, mouths, hands, and all our senses."[3] So the sermon leads to the Lord's Supper, and the Lord's Supper is an assurance and exhibition of the gospel promises that were just preached.

3. Offering

After the sermon is the "offertory," which begins with a collection of money for the support of the church and its ministry, including to the poor. The minister reads several of the offertory sentences (pp. 247-50), and while they are being read the offering is taken. The offertory sentences outline a theology of giving: why we give, and what we give—our money, but also our time and our hearts. But the sentences are not simply meant to inform you. They are meant to persuade us to take that knowledge and put it into action. Worship is not just fine words and fine feelings: by giving in proportion to our resources, we are demonstrating that we mean what we say.

The offertory continues with a prayer for the church (p. 250). It's a prayer not only for part of the church but for all Christians, with one limitation: it is "for the whole state of Christ's church militant here on earth." The distinction is between the "church militant" (here on earth fighting against sin and the devil), and the "church triumphant" (our brothers and sisters in heaven, no longer fighting these foes). The prayer book has many prayers for the church on earth, but none for the church in heaven, and purgatory is clearly rejected (Article 22, p. 637). This is one of the ways the prayer book distills the theology of the Reformation and puts it into liturgical form.

This prayer includes a petition for God "to direct and dispose the hearts of all Christian rulers." Earlier in the service we prayed for those in civil authority, whether Christian or not (p. 245). Here we are praying for the church, so this petition is for those members of the church who are called to public office, not just in one country but anywhere in the world.

In the prayer for the church we repeatedly ask God to give grace. The paragraph on page 251 starts "Give grace, O heavenly Father, to all bishops and pastors." Next is the whole church, both generally ("And to all thy people give thy heavenly grace") and specifically ("especially to this congregation here present"). And finally, remembering the saints who have gone before us, we ask that God would "give us grace so to follow their good examples." If God grants that request, which we ask in faith, we know we will some day pass from the church militant to the church triumphant, and "with them" we will "be partakers" of God's "heavenly kingdom."

A rubric set into the prayer on page 250 tells the priest whether to say the words about "our alms and oblations." That little detail is significant. *Oblation* means "offering" (p. 756). At this point in the medieval Mass, the bread and wine were offered to God; later in the service they would be consecrated, and from that point it was believed they were no longer bread and wine, but became Jesus Christ himself. After that, Christ himself (under the signs, or appearances, of bread and wine) was offered to God the Father as a sacrifice for sin. But the English reformers wanted to restore the scriptural emphasis on the Lord's Supper as a feast, a participation in the one sacrifice offered by Christ on the cross (Hebrews 10:11-14). They wanted to avoid any suggestion that the bread and wine were being offered to God as a sacrifice for sins. So the rubric tells the priest to say the words "alms and oblations," but only if a collection is taken for the poor and the church. Here it is our money, and then later in the service ourselves (p. 264), that we offer to God.

The service can end here. The first rubric on page 268 explains that on Sundays and holy days when the Lord's Supper is not celebrated, the first half of the Communion service should be read (meaning everything through p. 251, with a concluding collect and blessing from pp. 266-68). If the service ends here, it is called "Ante-Communion." For the first three hundred years of use of the Book of Common Prayer, in most Anglican churches the typical Sunday service was Morning Prayer, Litany, and Ante-Communion.

If the service does end here, then we will have heard the law and the gospel, listened to a sermon, offered our gifts, and prayed for the whole church militant. If the service does not end here, then all of this is immediate preparation for the most holy sacrament of our redemption. We hear the law and examine our heart to be ready for the sacrament; we hear the gospel and are filled with thanksgiving; we hear the word of Christ preached to be ready to receive the body and blood of Christ; and we give to the one who gives himself to us.

4. Communing

Now, if the service continues, we are ready to ascend still higher—all the way to heaven. Our ascent is carefully planned. It began with an exhortation the previous week, encouraging us to prepare (pp. 251-5), and with the law and gospel in the first part of the Communion service. This next part of the service can be divided into a "plateau" and an "ascent."

Let's start with the plateau. If we are going to climb a mountain, we need to spend some time on level ground preparing, to make sure we are ready for the steep climb ahead. It's the same idea here. This plateau (or "base camp") phase emphasizes two aspects of the spiritual preparation for this ascent: *repentance*, that is, being sincerely sorry for our sin and intending to turn from it and obey God; and *faith*, that is, trusting in Jesus Christ as the one who saves us from sin and gives us new life. Repentance and faith will appear in an exhortation, an invitation, a confession of sin, an absolution, and a set of Scripture verses that urge us forward. These parts of the service help us prepare for the ascent.

First, there is the exhortation. An exhortation is a warning to avoid something, or a strong encouragement to do something. Here it's both. The exhortation is read by the priest and it begins this way: "Dearly beloved in the Lord, ye that mind to come to the holy communion of the body and blood of our Saviour Christ must consider how Saint Paul exhorteth all persons diligently to prove and examine themselves, before they presume to eat of that bread and drink of that cup" (p. 255). This is a reference to 1 Corinthians 11:27-30. The exhortation goes on to lay out the sacramental theology expressed in the Communion service. To Christians who approach with "a true penitent heart" and "a lively faith" (or living, real faith), "the benefit is great." It is a "holy sacrament" in which "we spiritually eat the flesh of Christ and drink his blood"; "we dwell in Christ, and Christ in us." But if we receive the sacrament unworthily, that is, without repentance and faith, then it is not the benefit but the danger that is great. The exhortation spells out all this, with thanksgiving for the "exceeding great love" that Jesus Christ showed by "dying for us." At the end, the people respond "Amen" (p. 256).

Next, the priest reads the famous invitation to confession. It is addressed not to those who are perfect, but to those who are penitent ("truly and earnestly repent you of your sins") and who are committed to reconciliation with others ("are in love and charity with your neighbours") and personal holiness ("intend to lead a new life"). If that describes you, you're supposed to "draw near with faith" and "make your humble confession to almighty God, meekly kneeling upon your knees" (p. 257). And that is what the people do. They kneel down, and they stay kneeling until it is time to receive the bread and wine. But where exactly are the people kneeling?

If you have been to a Communion service where these words were read, the people probably knelt in their pews, and only came forward right before they received the bread and wine. But there are hints in the prayer book of an older Anglican practice. Right before the exhortation and invitation, any members of the congregation who were going to partake of the communion, called "communicants," would come forward into the chancel (p. 255). The chancel is the part of the church where the communion table is, historically the eastern end of the building set apart by a screen (*cancellus* in Latin) and reserved for the clergy. The priest would read the exhortation on pages 255-56 to those gathered in the chancel. And when he said "draw near" and "kneel" (p. 257), he meant it quite literally: the communicants had gathered in the chancel, and he was telling them to draw near to the communion table and kneel.

Not every church is built to accommodate this practice. But the symbolism is important. The chancel is like the upper room where Jesus gathered with his disciples for the Last Supper (Luke 22:12-13). It is like the holy of holies where the omnipresent God chooses to meet with his people (Exodus 26:33-34), where we now, by the blood of Christ, can "draw near" (Hebrews 10:19-22). The physical progression—moving into the chancel and toward the communion table—is parallel to the spiritual progression and ascent of the liturgy.

Kneeling, the people and priest say together the confession (p. 257). The confession in Morning and Evening Prayer picks up on the image of sin as a sickness, while the confession in Holy Communion draws on a different image. It is an image of sin found in the story of Cain, employed by the great Jewish commentator Rashi, and illustrated by *The Pilgrim's Progress*: the image of sin as a burden.[4] Disclosing our sins to God, we admit: "The remembrance of them is grievous unto us, The burden of them is intolerable."

Yet we ask God to sweep all this away: "For thy Son our Lord Jesus Christ's sake, Forgive us all this past." After this baring of our souls in the confession, the priest reads the absolution. It declares pardon and deliverance from "our heavenly Father" for all who turn to him in repentance and faith (p. 258).

This "plateau" phase ends with verses of Scripture from Jesus and the apostles Paul and John (p. 258), the most famous of which is John 3:16. These are called "The Comfortable Words," and the word *comfortable* has its older meaning of "to strengthen or encourage" (p. 750). These verses of Scripture, at the very end of the plateau, right before the ascent, give us the strength and conviction we need to go on. These verses urge us to remember that God loves us no matter how much we have sinned, and that Jesus died for us and was the "propitiation" for our sins. (*Propitiation* is in the glossary on page 758.) Jesus bids us to come, to "truly turn" to him. How can we refuse?

Now the ascent begins. The priest says: "Lift up your hearts." There is that word again—*hearts*. And we are supposed to lift them up. To where? The people respond: "We lift them up unto the Lord." And where is our Lord Jesus Christ? The answer to that question is the key to understanding the rest of the service.

Jesus is in heaven, where he ascended and where he sits, depicted as a king on his throne, until he returns at the final judgment. This is taught by many passages of Scripture (for example, Acts 2:34-36; Ephesians 1:20-23; Colossians 3:1-4; Hebrews 1:1-3, 13; 1 Peter 3:21-23). In the Articles of Religion, Article 4 says, "Christ did truly rise again from death, and took again his body, with flesh, bones, and all things appertaining to the perfection of man's nature, wherewith he ascended into heaven, and there sitteth until he return to judge all men at the last day" (p. 629; also the rubric on pp. 269-70). And if we, too, were to ascend to heaven, what would we hear? Whose songs, sweeter than any on earth, would be in our ears?

The priest turns toward the Lord's table and proclaims our duty to give thanks to God, and then says (or sings): "Therefore with angels and archangels, and with all the company of heaven, we laud and magnify thy glorious name, evermore praising thee and saying: 'Holy, holy, holy, Lord

God of hosts, heaven and earth are full of thy glory. Glory be to thee, O Lord Most High. Amen'" (p. 259). In many churches, the people join the priest in singing these words.

Remember that someone in the Bible, the prophet Isaiah, *was* caught up to heaven in a vision, and he saw the cherubim and seraphim and heard this very song (Isaiah 6:1-4). And how did he respond? He said he was unclean and unworthy (Isaiah 6:5). Which is exactly how we respond in the Communion service. Right after we hear the "Holy, holy, holy" of the angels, we say the prayer that begins "We do not presume to come to this thy table, O merciful Lord, trusting in our own righteousness, but in thy manifold and great mercies" (p. 261). This prayer, known as the Prayer of Humble Access, is one of the most beautiful and soul-stirring in the prayer book. Its plea is "that Communion should be a moment when this relationship of faith is strengthened and nourished, producing the desired fruit for eternity."[5]

Only one prayer remains before the communion: the Prayer of Consecration (p. 262). It recalls the death of Christ, that "full, perfect, and sufficient sacrifice, oblation, and satisfaction for the sins of the whole world." It asks that we who receive this bread and wine, "in remembrance of his death and passion, may be partakers of his body and blood." And it concludes with Jesus' words at the Last Supper: "Take, eat; this is my body which was given for you" and "Drink ye all of this." Our Lord commands us to eat this bread and drink this wine, to be partakers of his body and blood, and immediately we obey.[6]

The priest hands to each kneeling person a piece of bread, saying: "The body of our Lord Jesus Christ, which was given for thee, preserve thy body and soul unto everlasting life. Take and eat this in remembrance that Christ died for thee, and feed on him in thy heart by faith with thanksgiving" (p. 263). And the priest or an assistant gives each person the chalice, saying: "The blood of our Lord Jesus Christ, which was shed for thee, preserve thy body and soul unto everlasting life. Drink this in remembrance that Christ's blood was shed for thee, and be thankful" (p. 263). The personal intensity of these words is unmistakable: "Christ died for *thee*"; "Christ's blood was shed for *thee*."

Remember Bishop Jewel's question: If Christ is in heaven, and we are on earth, how can we ascend to him? In answering that question, Bishop Jewel drew on the Gospel of John and the work of many church fathers, including Augustine, Clement, Jerome, and Tertullian. He wrote:

> When we speak of the mystery of Christ, and of eating his body, we must shut up and abandon all our bodily senses. And as we cannot say that we see him with our bodily eyes, or hear him with our bodily ears, or touch him with our bodily feeling; so likewise we cannot, and therefore may not, say we taste him or eat him with our bodily mouth. In this work we must open all the inner and spiritual senses of our soul: so shall we not only see his body, but hear him, and feel him, and taste him, and eat him. This is the mouth and the feeling of faith. By the hand of faith we reach unto him, and by the mouth of faith we receive his body.[7]

Bishop Jewel's answer is the same one given in the Communion service. The priest said, "Lift up your hearts." The people responded: "We lift them up unto the Lord." We are guests at a heavenly feast (Hebrews 12:22-24), seeing with the eyes of faith (2 Kings 6:17; John 8:56). "Take and eat," said Jesus, and we do. Taking the bread and the chalice into our hands, eating the bread and drinking the wine with our mouths, we "feed on him in [our] heart by faith" (p. 263; also Articles 28 and 30, pp. 639-40). Then, as thankful guests who are lavishly welcomed into the Father's house, we say: "Our Father, who art in heaven" (p. 264).

This is the highest point in the prayer book—our entrance by faith into the holy of holies where Christ has gone before us (Hebrews 10:11-22). That is why everything happened in the plateau—repentance, because we are in the presence of a holy God; and faith, because only by faith can we see the risen Christ (John 20:29; 1 Corinthians 13:12). This sacrament is a memorial of a sacrifice, "a perpetual memory" of our Savior's "precious death until his coming again" (p. 262). But it is not a bare memorial. In the communion "the body of Christ is given, taken, and eaten . . . after a heavenly and spiritual manner" (Article 28, p. 640). By taking and eating this bread and drinking this wine we are actually made "partakers of his most precious body and blood" (p. 262, paraphrasing 1 Corinthians 10:16).

5. *Thanksgiving*

The service comes quickly to an end. But just as the ascent was carefully orchestrated by the prayer book, so is the descent. As we approached the Lord's table in repentance and faith, so we leave it with praise and thanksgiving to God, who has fed our souls and filled us with his peace.

The priest says one of the two post-Communion prayers, in which we offer ourselves to God in thanksgiving and awe (pp. 264-65). Then the people and priest say or sing the *Gloria in Excelsis.* This ancient Christian hymn goes back to at least the 300s, and it extols the Trinity. It begins with the words of the angels announcing the birth of Christ: "Glory be to God on high, and on earth peace, good will toward men" (Luke 2:14). With these words, it is as if we are leaving heaven with hearts full of praise and with a song of the angels on our lips. And just as the angels (literally, "messengers") brought the good news of Christ to the shepherds, so we leave the liturgy bearing the message that Christ is Lord. Next might be one more prayer, one of the collects that sum up all the preceding prayers (pp. 266-68).

Then come the final words of the service. When we started the service, we prayed in the Collect for Purity that we would "perfectly love" God (p. 242). That love has animated our responses at every point of the service, all the way down to our offering God "ourselves, our souls and bodies, to be a reasonable, holy, and lively sacrifice" (p. 264). We have heard the Scriptures both read and preached, learning and relearning about God's work for us and in us.

This is a good beginning. But what next? What is it that will sustain us in knowing and loving God? The divine gift of peace. "The peace of God" does not simply mean the absence of conflict, but wholeness and fullness. Morning and Evening Prayer teach that God is the "author of peace" (p. 14), "that peace which the world cannot give" (p. 24). The gift of this peace, from the giver of all good gifts, is how the Communion service ends. The priest blesses the people, declaring to them: "The peace of God, which passeth all understanding, keep your hearts and minds in the knowledge and love of God, and of his Son Jesus Christ our Lord. And the blessing of God almighty, the Father, the Son, and the Holy Ghost, be amongst you and remain with you always." And all God's people say, "Amen."

7

Reading the Bible with the Prayer Book

✝

IMAGINE A DAY IN LATE MAY 1549. A churchwarden has just received from the book binder this bulky new volume, the Book of Common Prayer. As he opens it and turns past the title page and the table of contents, the first thing he comes to is the preface. Later on, in the 1662 Book of Common Prayer, this would be called "Concerning the Service of the Church" (p. xiii), but in 1549 it was simply "The Preface." This was Archbishop Cranmer's chance to explain what the new prayer book was all about.

How would you have justified the new Book of Common Prayer? Would you have started by talking about the prayers being in English? Or by invoking royal authority? Would you have talked about the new Reformation emphasis on the people receiving the bread and wine?

Or on how the sacrament is understood as a spiritual and heavenly feast?

That's not how Archbishop Cranmer begins. He starts with reading the Bible. In the early church, Cranmer said, the Bible was read through. It wasn't just for the clergy. The people were meant, "by daily hearing of holy Scripture read in the church," to "continually profit more and more in the knowledge of God and be the more inflamed with the love of his true religion" (p. xiv). But in Cranmer's day, that was not done. The Scriptures were read disjointedly, here a bit, there a bit. It was a challenge just to find out what was supposed to be read. The flow of the reading was interrupted by liturgical responses. Most important of all, when the Scriptures were read, they were not in English. There were so many barriers to the people understanding the life-giving word of God.

These problems were precisely the ones that Cranmer said the Book of Common Prayer would solve. Now, he said, there was a calendar that was "plain and easy to be understood" (p. xv). No longer would a steady stream of interruptions "break the continual course of the reading of the Scripture" (p. xv). At last the public reading of the Scriptures would be in English.

The preface is a manifesto for the Book of Common Prayer as a means of reading the Bible. There were some adjustments between Cranmer's original design in 1549 and the 1662 revision of the prayer book, but this central purpose has remained the same. The result is that the prayer book gives us a feast of Bible reading, and the way the readings are ordered shows deep theological and psychological insight.

This chapter explains how to read the Bible with the Book of Common Prayer. It walks through the three different systems of Bible reading in the prayer book: one for every day, and two for Sundays. That may seem complicated, but it has a reason and a rhythm. And once you begin, it will be easy to keep going.

THE DAILY READINGS

The first system of Bible reading in the Book of Common Prayer is the daily readings. Every morning there are two readings, and every evening there are two readings. To find the readings is usually simplicity itself: you look them up in the calendar, which is organized by the civil year, January to December. The calendar starts on page xxxiv.

On certain red-letter days, you'll see a dash in the calendar instead of a reading. That directs you to look at the tables right before the calendar to find a special reading for that day. Those tables are on page xxxi ("Mattins," or Morning Prayer) and page xxxii ("Evensong," or Evening Prayer). There are also a few days in those tables that have variable dates, such as Good Friday.

The basic pattern for the daily readings is that we are reading the Scriptures in sequence. We read Genesis 1, then Genesis 2, then Genesis 3, then Genesis 4. It's not a snippet here and a few verses over there. We're reading the Bible straight through. And because it's a chapter at a time, in order, the 1662 lectionary is especially easy to use.

There are exceptions to this pattern of continuous reading, but they are exceptions. Day after day, the Book of Common

Prayer takes us through the Bible. Continuous reading is supposed to make it easier to understand what the authors and the Author are saying. "Faith cometh by hearing" (Romans 10:17 KJV), but this hearing is not just a cascade of words falling on our ears, or a stream of printed letters before our eyes, without any understanding. It is a core Reformation principle that the word of God is meant to be understood, that its critical points are truly accessible, that its message is transformative.

If you are used to reading the Bible but are new to the Book of Common Prayer, you are in for a surprise. Instead of reading all of the Bible through exactly once in a year, we read almost all of the New Testament three times, and the great majority of the Old Testament one time, but there are also things we do not read: some of the genealogies, some of the ceremonial law from Exodus and Leviticus, the two books of Chronicles (which cover much of the same ground as Kings), one chapter of Proverbs, the Song of Solomon, and some of the apocalyptic literature from Ezekiel and Revelation. Why?

The key is that Morning and Evening Prayer aren't simply "private devotions." Although they can be read by one family or person, these services are designed to be read by a minister with the congregation, without a sermon. So the question is what Scriptures are going to edify the church when read publicly, without the exposition that would be needed to extract the nectar from some of these passages. That principle helps explain the omissions from the daily readings.

The Psalms are not included in the daily table of lessons. They are read through even more often—every month—not as lessons to hear but as expressions of praise, as discussed in chapter three. One author has said the Psalms are "to be read once a month, the Bible once a year, rather like a good running clock where the Psalms, the minute hand, go round quickly within the slower pattern of the hours, the Scripture."[1]

You might be in for another surprise in the daily lessons: we read the Apocrypha. These books, also called the deuterocanonical books, are not in the Hebrew Bible. But they were included in the Greek translations of the Jewish Scriptures widely used in the time of Christ (commonly called the Septuagint). The apocryphal books were well-known to the writers of the New Testament, who make many allusions to them. Several examples are Luke 1:52 echoing Sirach 10:14; Romans 9:21 echoing Wisdom 15:7; and Hebrews 1:3 echoing Wisdom 7:26.

Since the earliest centuries after Christ, these books have also been read in church. There was a vigorous debate about whether they had the same divine authority as the rest of the Bible, dividing Saint Augustine on one side (yes) and Saint Jerome on the other (no). What was not in dispute, though, was whether to read these books in church.

At the Reformation, the debate over their status was revived. Eventually, at the Council of Trent, the Roman Catholic Church settled on the position that the books of the Apocrypha should be regarded as being the same as the Old and New Testament. By contrast, the Church of England, like the Lutherans and some of the Continental

Reformed, continued to read these books in church, even while carefully distinguishing them. These books were included in the King James Version of the Bible and its predecessors, including the Geneva Bible—in fact, most printings of the King James Version contained these books until the 1800s.

The English reformers took the position that the apocryphal books are read "for example of life and instruction of manners," but are not read "to establish any doctrine" (Article 6, p. 630). Because these books are not treated as canonical Scripture like the Old and New Testaments, they are not authoritative for the doctrine of the church. But they are not simply histories of what happened between the testaments. In fact, the historical books called Maccabees, which give the history of the Jewish revolt against Greek oppressors, are not read in the daily lessons. Instead, in the prayer book the Apocrypha is read for example and instruction, as a kind of Wisdom literature. Books like the Wisdom of Solomon and Sirach (also called Ecclesiasticus) are shrewd, sharp-witted, filled with insights about how to live a virtuous life. That explains why these books, along with Proverbs, Ecclesiastes, and Job, tend to be appointed for saints' days and why they are read in Trinitytide, the season of the year focused on teaching the ethical implications of the gospel.

THE COMMUNION READINGS

The second system of readings is for Communion, as a second service after Morning Prayer. This system provides two additional readings for Sundays and red-letter days. The first is an "epistle," usually from one of the New Testament epistles, but about a quarter of the time it is taken from Acts, Revelation, or the prophetic books of the Old Testament. The second reading is a "gospel," which is always from one of the four gospels. These epistles and gospels are printed in their entirety in the prayer book beginning on page 49.

The goals of these two systems of Bible reading are quite different. The daily readings are supposed to provide broad coverage, systematically taking us through book after book. But the Communion epistles and gospels are short (except in the week before Easter when the four accounts of the crucifixion are read). The Communion readings also connect with the church year, underscoring the themes for each day or season (as illustrated in chapters eight and nine of this book). As they are unfolded in sermons year after year, these short readings are supposed to work their way deep into our souls, rooting and establishing our faith.

Still another difference between the daily readings and the Communion readings is how far back these two systems go. The daily readings were set up at the Reformation by Archbishop Cranmer, with only minor adjustments in the 1662 Book of Common Prayer. But the Communion readings are much older. Most of the epistles and gospels have been read in church for at least thirteen centuries, and many can be traced back even to the 500s, to the time of Gregory the Great. On any given Sunday, the epistle and gospel readings in the Book of Common Prayer are usually the same ones that were read in the court of Charlemagne and the court of Elizabeth I, the same ones Thomas Aquinas and Martin

Luther preached on, and the same ones Johann Sebastian Bach wrote cantatas for.

By contrast, there are no such ancient roots for the three-year lectionaries in late-modern prayer books. Their dates of origin are years like 1979, or 1994, or 2019. They try to achieve the goals of both of the 1662 systems of Bible reading—broad coverage *and* thematic connection with the church year—all within one cycle of readings. But the iron law of lectionaries is that if you try to do everything, it's hard to do anything well. There's wisdom in how Archbishop Cranmer saw the daily readings and the Communion readings as having different, complementary purposes.

THE SUNDAY OLD TESTAMENT READINGS

There's one more system of Bible reading in the prayer book, added in 1561 by Archbishop Matthew Parker at Elizabeth I's instruction. This is a system of Old Testament readings only for Sundays. These are called "Sunday first lessons" because they displace the first lesson at Morning and Evening Prayer. The Sunday first lessons begin in Advent with Isaiah, which is read through Christmas and Epiphany. Then, beginning on Septuagesima (which always falls in January or February), the Sunday first lessons start with Genesis and proceed to give highlights from the Pentateuch, the histories of the judges and kings, the prophets, and finally selections from the Book of Proverbs. You can find these lessons in the table on page xxix.

The advantage of the Sunday first lessons is that they give an overview of the Old Testament to someone only coming to church on Sundays and red-letter days. A person who was hearing the daily readings would already be exposed to most of the Old Testament every year, but not everyone was doing that. Someone who heard the Old Testament only twice a week at church—hearing a couple chapters and then missing the next dozen—would struggle to follow the thread.

The disadvantage is that if you *are* participating in Morning and Evening Prayer every day, then your reading through the Scriptures in sequence is disrupted by the Sunday first lessons. But in the long run, because Sundays fall on different days from year to year, whatever you miss one year will be read the next. The judgment of Queen Elizabeth and Archbishop Parker was that the advantage of the new Sunday first lessons was weightier.

One purpose for the Sunday first lessons is biblical literacy. There is an emphasis on the ethical requirements of the law, especially with readings from Deuteronomy; and on wisdom, with extensive readings from Proverbs. And there is an emphasis on stories and prophecies that anticipate the Messiah, such as the fall of Adam and Eve, the sacrifice of Isaac, the blessings of Balaam, the songs of Deborah and Hannah, and the battle of David and Goliath. It's not surprising that many of the most gripping stories of the Old Testament are found here.

A further purpose for these lessons is to reinforce the Communion readings and the themes of the church year. Isaiah's prophecies of the coming Messiah are read before and throughout Christmastide. The deliverance from Pharaoh is read at Easter, when God delivers his people from the last enemy, Death. Deuteronomy is read around Ascension, as the new king gives his people the gift of the law. The warnings and examples of the kings and prophets are apt for the season of Trinity, as we think about how to walk with integrity and holiness. Often the connections between the Sunday first lessons and the Communion readings are even more specific and striking (for example, the Fifth Sunday in Lent, as discussed in chapter eight).

A final purpose is to teach us how to read the Scriptures, and in particular to teach us how to read the Old Testament. The telltale signs are the two books that are "out of order," in terms of the canonical order in English Bibles. Isaiah is moved to the beginning, and Proverbs is moved to the end. Why? Isaiah is especially remarkable for its many detailed predictions of the Messiah, including his birth and passion. Beginning with Isaiah tells the reader to look for Christ as we read the Old Testament. As we read of the failures of the patriarchs and judges, the kings and prophets, we should recognize our own failures and turn to Christ. This is the "pedagogical" use of the law (discussed in chapter six). The law reveals that we cannot keep God's commandments, and thus drives us to Christ.

Remember that another use of God's law is "moral." The law guides our actions and teaches us what it means to love God and neighbor (Matthew 22:37-40), showing us the life that is truly blessed (Psalm 1). That use of the law is emphasized by ending the year with Sunday lessons from Proverbs. As we read highlights of the Old Testament, going from Genesis through Habakkuk, "these stories of sin and judgment are also supposed to work on our moral imagination, to guide and form our intention for obedience. For that purpose, the pithy axioms found in Proverbs are invaluable. When placed at the end of the entire year's reading, the Proverbs reveal and sum up wisdom from the narratives."[2]

This sequence is a liturgical demonstration of justification by faith alone, followed by the fruit of faith, a righteous life: beginning with Isaiah we learn that Jesus Christ has come to save us, and ending with Proverbs we learn about how to live wisely as the children of God. Justification, then sanctification. And in between we have the great events and dramas of the Old Testament, showing us our need of salvation from sin and judgment (read in light of Isaiah) and teaching us how to live in this world (read in anticipation of Proverbs).

So the Sunday first lessons give us an overview of the Old Testament, reinforce the Communion readings as we walk through the church year, and teach us how to read the Bible. To achieve so much in a single set of Old Testament readings is a daunting and seemingly impossible task. Archbishop Parker did his work very well.

READING THE BIBLE
FROM THREE PERSPECTIVES

These three systems of Bible reading—the daily lessons, the Communion readings, and the Sunday first lessons—all work together. The daily readings lay a foundation of biblical literacy. This is how we learn what's in the Bible, from cover to cover. The Communion readings are short but deep. They teach us the essential doctrines of the church, emphasizing the life of Christ, and our life in Christ. And the Sunday first lessons give us the high points of the Old Testament, not only marking out the long sweep of the narrative from the patriarchs to the prophets, but also teaching us how to read the Old Testament in light of the New. We read it for Christ, finding him in the pages of Isaiah at the start of the year. But we do not want to be like a person who looks in a mirror and walks away unchanged (James 1:23-24). We want the word of God to change us from the inside out, for the fear of the Lord is the beginning of wisdom (Proverbs 9:10).

8

The Prayer Book and the Christian Year

✝

HOW DOES A WRITER CAPTURE our attention? How does a speaker persuade us to listen? Usually by promising us something new. But imagine a speaker who starts by saying "You already know this." That's how the Second Epistle of Peter begins. The apostle Peter tells his readers, "I shall keep reminding you of all this, although you know it and are well-grounded in the truth you possess" (2 Peter 1:12 REB). And again: "I have been recalling to you what you already know" (2 Peter 3:1 REB). This simple idea is at the heart of the church calendar: we need to recall what we already know.

Remembrance was central to the life of ancient Israel. In the Old Testament, Israel is faithful when Israel remembers; and when Israel forgets, Israel is unfaithful. Memory of what God has done for his people in the past is both the foundation of present faith and the matrix of future hope. There were annual feasts like Passover and annual fasts like the Day of Atonement, and the Old Testament even describes the observance of these kinds of days and seasons as a reason for the divine creation of the sun and moon (Genesis 1:14; Psalm 104:19). Beyond the biblical feasts and fasts, this impulse to mark events in annual patterns is just deeply human. In yearly cycles we remember birthdays, wedding anniversaries, and national holidays.

In a similar way, the church year prompts us to call to mind annually the central events and truths of the Christian faith. This is not simply remembering as opposed to forgetting, but it is also a public celebration, proclaiming the great deeds of the Lord (compare 1 Corinthians 11:26). John Davenant, the Bishop of Salisbury (1621–1641), describes it this way: "It was piously and prudently provided by the ancient fathers that those great benefits of the incarnation, the passion, the resurrection, and ascension of the Son of God, and the descent of the Holy Spirit, should be celebrated annually in the church."[1] We remember these days "by stated anniversaries," Davenant continues, "'lest,' as Augustine says, 'in the rolling wheel of time an ungrateful forgetfulness creep upon us.'"[2]

Each feast and fast is like a time capsule buried for us by the church. As we open each one, we are reminded that God has done great things for us (Psalm 126:2).

THE TWO HALVES OF THE CHURCH YEAR

The church year has two halves. The first is about the incarnation and the great events by which God has accomplished our salvation. The second half is about how we live as Christians. This shift from salvation to sanctification occurs in many of the epistles. The apostle Paul will typically start with doctrine about our salvation in Christ, and then say "Therefore" and launch into the implications for how we live (for example, Romans 12:1).

The incarnation half of the year begins with Advent and runs through Christmas, Epiphany, the 'Gesimas, Lent, Easter, Ascension, and Whitsunday (also called Pentecost). It is roughly from the start of December through May or early June. One common misunderstanding is that in these seasons we're engaged in a mythic, cyclical repetition of the life of Christ. In other words, in some sense Jesus is born anew every Christmas or resurrected again every Easter. (One of us was once told not to say alleluias in Lent because Jesus wasn't risen from the dead yet!) But Christianity confesses that our Lord has already come to save us—dying, rising again, and ascending—and that he is now reigning until he comes again to judge the world. The first half of the church year isn't a way to repeat these events. It's a way the church commemorates them and teaches their significance.

The other half of the year is a season called "Trinity" or "Trinitytide" because it begins with Trinity Sunday. It is roughly from May or early June through November. We could say that the first half of the year is about the life of Christ, and the second half is about our life in Christ. George Herbert (1593-1633), rector of a rural English parish and author of religious poems that are read to this day, described these two halves of the church year as God's "two rare cabinets full of treasure, / The *Trinity*, and *Incarnation*."[3] But these treasures are not locked up or out of reach. Addressing God, Herbert writes:

> Thou hast unlockt them both,
> And made them jewels to betroth
> The work of thy creation
> Unto thy self in everlasting pleasure.

These treasures remind us that Jesus Christ has made us, the church, his bride. The annual round of feasts and fasts are our engagement ring.

INCARNATION: THE FIRST HALF OF THE CHURCH YEAR

The first half of the year contains two cycles. The Nativity Cycle is centered on the birth of Christ, and the Easter Cycle on his passion, resurrection, and ascension.

The Nativity Cycle. Nativity means "birth." The Nativity Cycle begins with the season of Advent, which starts on the Sunday nearest November 30 (Saint Andrew's Day). Its name comes from the Latin word *advenire*, which means "arrive." This season prepares us for the arrival of the Messiah. But not just one arrival. The Advent season has a double focus: the first advent and the second advent.

One of the unusual things about Advent in the prayer book is that it has a collect that is said through the whole season, tying it together. The collect mentions the two comings of Christ—he "came to visit us in great humility," but he will "come again in his glorious majesty, to judge both the quick and the dead" (p. 49). These themes of humility and judgment run through all the epistles and gospels of Advent.

Right after the four Sundays in Advent is December 25: "The Nativity of our Lord, or the Birthday of Christ, commonly called Christmas Day" (p. 57). The collect points us to the news we so joyfully celebrate at Christmas: the Son of God is made the Son of Man, so the children of men might become the children of God. And it draws a spiritual lesson. We must be born again—that is, we must become "regenerate and made thy children by adoption and grace" (p. 57).

At first, in the East the birth of Christ was celebrated on January 6. But by the 400s the December 25 date became widely used throughout both the East and the West. It is unlikely that the December 25 date was taken from a pagan holiday. The more likely explanation for the date lies in a widespread belief at the time that great events would recur on the same date, along with a tradition that Jesus died on March 25. So it was thought that the announcement of Jesus' birth to Mary was also on March 25, and nine months after that would be December 25.[4]

Whatever the exact origin of the date, the celebration of Jesus' birth goes back to the first couple centuries after Christ. Even so, there have sometimes been Christians who didn't think we should celebrate Christmas—famously, the Pilgrims who left England and landed at Plymouth, founding the Massachusetts Bay Colony. They believed that only the weekly Sabbath (Sunday) was authorized by the Bible. You probably don't need much convincing to think Christmas is a good idea.

But you might need more convincing to celebrate the next major feast day: the Circumcision of Christ. Jesus was a Jewish boy born to a Jewish mother. According to Old Testament law, that meant that on the eighth day after his birth, he had to be circumcised. January 1 is the eighth day, counting Christmas Day itself. The collect emphasizes the perfect keeping of the law: "Almighty God, who madest thy blessed Son to be circumcised and obedient to the law for man" (p. 66). This act of obedience and blood-shedding foreshadows his passion when "he humbled himself, and became obedient unto death, even the death of the cross" (Philippians 2:8 KJV).

You might be in the habit of thinking of January 1 as a day for resolutions for the new year, a day to think about what you've failed at and want to do better. There's nothing wrong with that. But this feast points us to something grace-filled: Jesus Christ has already kept the law for you. This useful and soul-nourishing feast was retained at the Reformation not only by the Church of England but also by the Lutheran churches and some of the Reformed churches on the Continent (see, for example, Article 67 of the Synod of Dort).

But is Jesus a savior only for part of mankind? Only for Jews? Or also for Gentiles? If that question is raised by the feast of the Circumcision, it is answered by the next festival, which comes on January 6: "The Epiphany, or the Manifestation of Christ to the Gentiles" (p. 68). *Epiphany* means "manifestation." This is a very old feast, going back to at least around AD 200 in Egypt, and adopted in the West by around AD 400.

In the tradition of the church, three biblical stories are especially connected to Epiphany. One is the arrival of the wise men, the first Gentiles to appear in the Christmas story. Another is the baptism of Jesus, when he was declared by the Father to be the Son of God. The third is the miracle at Cana, when Jesus turned water into wine, which was "the first of the signs which revealed his glory" (John 2:11 REB). The Book of Common Prayer has all three stories read on Epiphany.

But what was Jesus revealed *for*? There are clues in the Epiphany collect. It asks "that we, who know thee now by faith, may after this life have the fruition of thy glorious Godhead" (p. 68). *Fruition* means "enjoyment" (p. 752). Yet we are sinful—as we're reminded by the virgin birth, since Jesus could not have a human father and inherit Adam's sinful nature; and as we're reminded by Jesus' perfect keeping of the law, since it's something we cannot do. So Epiphany makes us wonder. How can we, though sinful, know God? How can we, though sinful, attain to the enjoyment of God's very being and "be partakers of the divine nature" (2 Peter 1:4 KJV)? The answers are coming in the next cycle.

Forty days after Christmas Day, on February 2, comes the last feast of the Nativity Cycle: the Presentation of Christ in the Temple. Like the circumcision, the presentation was an act of obedience to the law. As the Virgin Mary and Joseph offered the sacrifice prescribed for a first-born son

(Exodus 13:2, 12-15), the infant Jesus was recognized as the Christ by two witnesses, prophets awaiting the day of his coming (as told in the gospel of the day). An alternative name for this feast is the Purification of the Blessed Virgin Mary because under the Old Testament law, after the birth of a male son there was a forty-day time of purification for the mother (Leviticus 12). In the collect we are presented to God, like the Christ Child, and we are cleansed from spiritual impurity, as the Virgin Mary was purified according to the Law of Moses: we pray to be "presented unto thee with pure and clean hearts." The collect also reminds us that this infant is the incarnate Son of God—"thy only-begotten Son was this day presented in the temple in the substance of our flesh" (p. 211). Still another name for this day is Candlemas, because of an old custom of carrying lighted candles to church on this day, perhaps because of Simeon's words in the gospel: "For mine eyes have seen thy salvation, which thou hast prepared before the face of all people, a light to lighten the Gentiles, and the glory of thy people Israel." Now the Nativity Cycle is drawing to an end.

The Easter Cycle. The incarnation half of the church year has a second cycle, which directs our attention to the great events that are the reason God became man. In this cycle, all the major feast and fast days circle around Easter (p. xxiv). The date of Easter varies from year to year because it is tied to the date of Passover, and thus to the lunar calendar. There is a table on page xxvi that shows how to work out the date of Easter, but fair warning—it is not for the faint of heart.

Just as the Nativity Cycle began with a season of preparation (Advent), the Easter Cycle begins with a season of preparation, the forty days of Lent. But first there is preparation for the preparation! This is the pre-Lent season called the 'Gesimas, pronounced *JEZ-i-muhs*. This odd name comes from the titles of three Sundays: Septuagesima (Latin for "seventieth"), Sexagesima ("sixtieth"), and Quinquagesima ("fiftieth"). It's only a rough correlation, but these Sundays are approximately seventy days, sixty days, and fifty days before Easter.

Lent is a season of discipline, as we look forward to Christ's passion and resurrection. Many people think of Lent as a time to curry favor with God, to let go of a small indulgence like chocolate, or to just try harder. But Gesimatide offers a different path to Lent. On these three Sundays, the epistles and gospels underline perseverance and grace (p. 81), humility and faith (p. 83), and charity and mercy (p. 85). These are not lessons about pulling ourselves up by our bootstraps, or balancing out the debits and credits in a ledger kept by God. These readings teach kingdom values—about salvation by grace alone, about hearing and responding to the word of God with faith, about no work being good if it is not done with love.

Right after the 'Gesimas comes the First Day of Lent. Popularly known as "Ash Wednesday," this is the only day in the entire year that has its own special service in the prayer book. The seven penitential psalms, which since ancient times have been associated with repentance and sorrow for sin, are all read on this day: Psalms 6, 32, 38, 51, 102, 130, and 143 (pp. xxxiii, 357). And Ash Wednesday introduces the collect that is used all through Lent (p. 87). The only other season with its own collect is Advent, another time of preparation.

What we won't find anywhere in the Book of Common Prayer for this day is ashes. In fact, no Anglican prayer book included ashes for Ash Wednesday until the 1970s. How could this be?

The answer lies in the special Ash Wednesday service called the "Commination." That word means "threatening," and right at the beginning of the service there is a set of searing curses for everyone who fails to keep the law. These are drawn mostly from Deuteronomy 27, but also from other Old and New Testament passages. These curses fall especially on sins against the needy and vulnerable (for example, "Cursed is he that maketh the blind to go out of his way"), as well as sins of the heart (for example, "Cursed is he that putteth his trust in man, and taketh man for his defence, and in his heart goeth from the Lord"). During this recitation of the curses, the congregation is not left passive. Instead it is tugged toward agreeing with the just requirements of the law of God: after each curse, the congregation says "Amen." Next comes a short evangelistic homily, which begins with haunting imagery of divine judgment, but then turns halfway through to extol the grace and mercy offered to sinners in Jesus Christ.[5]

What comes next in the Commination service is a dramatic moment: the priest walks out of the chancel, joining the congregation in kneeling and saying Psalm 51, David's great prayer of confession after he committed adultery and murder. This deeply moving psalm ends with the joy of a forgiven sinner. Then come more prayers, ending with blessing and peace. And then Holy Communion.

Commination and Communion set the tone for Lent. These services are serious about sin and serious about forgiveness. When we leave, we aren't carrying on our faces a reminder of mortality. Instead, we begin the Lenten journey with the joy of the prodigal child who once was lost but now is found. We have been brought to the Father's table.

The collect introduced on the First Day of Lent strikes all the keynotes of this season (p. 87). It has God's great love for us ("who hatest nothing that thou hast made"); his welcome for all penitent sinners ("who . . . dost forgive the sins of all those who are penitent"); our request not merely for external reformation but for the divine gift of a new heart ("Create and make in us new and contrite hearts"); our need of divine mercy because of our sins ("worthily lamenting our sins and acknowledging our wretchedness"); and God's rich supply of that mercy ("may obtain of thee, the God of all mercy, perfect remission and forgiveness").

This is how a prayer-book Lent begins: as a season for those who know they are loved, for those who have already mourned their sins and received God's forgiveness. If we start Lent this way, we'll still give things up. It *is* forty days of fasting. But how we begin changes how we continue.

But why does the prayer book tell us when to fast? In fact, you might remember from chapter two that one of the flashpoints for the Reformation was a Swiss reformer, Huldrych

Zwingli, serving sausages during Lent and arguing that fasting should be voluntary. So why isn't fasting up to each one of us?

That was a question George Herbert took up in another poem. Herbert's readers already knew that Jesus taught the importance of fasting. In the Sermon on the Mount, he said to his disciples: "when you give to the needy," "when you pray," and "when you fast" (Matthew 6:2, 5, 16 ESV). But that still leaves the question of *when*, and specifically of who decides when. That is what Herbert addresses in his poem "Lent," which begins this way:

> Welcome dear feast of Lent: who loves not thee,
> He loves not Temperance, or Authority,
> But is compos'd of passion.

> The Scriptures bid us *fast*; the Church says, *now*:
> Give to thy Mother, what thou wouldst allow
> To ev'ry Corporation.[6]

To control our passions, we need temperance (that is, restraint). But developing that virtue is easier when we have someone training us, and that is exactly what happens in Lent. Prescribed for our good, Lent is a gift given to us by Mother Church. (When Herbert analogizes Mother Church to a *Corporation*, the word has its older meaning of a group of people organized for a purpose, not just a business.) To use another analogy, we are like a team of nine-year-old baseball players who need a coach to schedule a practice so we all show up at the same time to run through catching fly balls. Left to our own devices, it might not happen.

Of course not all churches observe this season, but Lent and other fast days are prescribed by churches in the Anglican tradition. The Articles of Religion teach that churches can make rules for things like feast and fast days, as long as they are not inconsistent with the Scriptures (Article 20, p. 636). And these rules, when given to us by proper authorities, should be followed (Article 34, p. 642).

With that background, it's easier to understand what the Book of Common Prayer says about fasting. It says to fast on the forty days of Lent, except for Sundays, which are always feast days. All the feasts and fasts are listed on pages xxiv-xxv. When you see the reference to the "even" or "vigil" of certain days, that means the day before—like Christmas Eve before Christmas.

The traditional ways of observing a prayer-book Lent are fasting, almsgiving, and prayer. Fasting would typically be abstaining from rich foods, such as meat, and taking the money that was saved and giving it as alms for the poor. As for prayer, Thomas Ken, an English bishop known today for writing the Doxology, recommended for extra Lenten devotions the daily reading of Psalm 51 and the Litany. But the Book of Common Prayer does not spell out the details.

However you keep the fast of Lent, remember to approach it in the spirit that the 'Gesimas taught you. If we look back to the very first day of preparation, Septuagesima (p. 81), we'll see that the epistle reminds us that the point of self-discipline is to persevere in the faith (1 Corinthians 9:24-27). And the gospel for Septuagesima is the parable of the workers in the vineyard, who all received the same pay no matter how long they worked (Matthew 20:1-16). It is all grace, all the time.

There are six Sundays in Lent, and the last is "The Sunday next before Easter." In the Middle Ages it was often called "Palm Sunday," a title revived in many Protestant churches in the late twentieth century. But the title used by the Book of Common Prayer is quite intentional, and it points us toward a different and more ancient way of thinking about this day. Instead of being about the triumphal entry of Jesus into Jerusalem, it looks toward the suffering and also the exaltation of Jesus. We could almost say it's a glimpse of the triumphal entry into *heaven*.

The proof is in the proper readings. The epistle is Philippians 2:5-11, which describes the humbling of the Son of God to take on our flesh, a prelude to his exaltation over every name and power. The second lesson at Morning Prayer is Matthew 26 and the gospel is Matthew 27:1-54. Together these readings are the passion account in the Gospel According to Saint Matthew, ending with the words of the Roman centurion: "Truly this was the Son of God."

In making the crucifixion and not the triumphal entry into Jerusalem the focus of this Sunday, the Book of Common Prayer follows many centuries of church tradition. Since at least the 600s in Rome, and perhaps earlier, Matthew 26 and 27 have been read on this Sunday. That pattern continued for nearly a thousand years to the Reformation, and long after that in Anglican and Lutheran churches. It was for this Sunday that Johann Sebastian Bach wrote his "Saint Matthew's Passion," which includes the text of Matthew 26 and 27.

The rest of this week leading up to Easter, called "Passion Week" or "Holy Week," is about the cross. We see the passion of our Savior through the eyes of all four gospel writers. The epistles and the Old Testament passages appointed for epistle readings are also about the cross. One of those, on the Thursday before Easter—the night of the Last Supper—is the account of Jesus' institution of the holy sacrament of his body and blood (1 Corinthians 11:17-34).

Throughout this week, two collects are said every day: the collect for the Sunday next before Easter and the collect for Lent (p. 100). Together these collects keep our attention on the cross, for it reveals God's "tender love towards mankind" and is the means by which he "forgive[s] the sins of all those who are penitent."

This week before Easter culminates in Good Friday. The collects remember the death of Christ, and plead with God to see the church as his own family for whom Christ died, and to turn the hearts of all who are outside of the church. The readings fix our sight on the sacrifice of the Beloved Son (Genesis 22:1-19), the Suffering Servant (Isaiah 53), the Crucified One (John 18; 19:1-37). The epistle provides God's own interpretation of this event as the culmination of all the Old Testament sacrifices in "the offering of the body of Jesus Christ once for all" (Hebrews 10:1-25 KJV). Here we see the love of God beyond all imagining. As a hymnwriter put it, paraphrasing the collect for Passion Week, with its themes of love, death, and incarnation:

My song is love unknown,
my Savior's love to me,

123

love to the loveless shown
that they might lovely be.
Oh, who am I,
that for my sake
my Lord should take
frail flesh and die?

The last reading for Good Friday, the second lesson at Evening Prayer, pulls together all these meditations on the death of Christ, asking how we should live in light of Christ's example of patient endurance in suffering (1 Peter 2). Following our Lord's example is another theme of the collect said throughout this week.

The next day is "Easter Even." The Book of Common Prayer does not have a long Easter Vigil service on the Saturday night before Easter. Instead, this day is quiet stillness, with none of the intensity of Good Friday or Easter Day. It is the stillness of the grave.

The Easter Even readings are short. They tell of Jesus' burial (Luke 23:50-56; Matthew 27:57-66), and promise that God will appear to deliver his people (Zechariah 9), and that he will lead them (Exodus 13—note the bones of Joseph as a sign of the promise of God's salvation in verse 19). The epistle is a central text on the descent of Christ into hell (1 Peter 3:17-22), and it connects our baptism to the death and resurrection of Jesus.

All these points are drawn together in the collect for Easter Even (p. 133). It looks back to Good Friday and reminds us of our baptism—"as we are baptized into the death of thy blessed Son, our Saviour Jesus Christ"—and looks forward to Easter Day—"that through the grave, and gate of death, we may pass to our joyful resurrection." The Easter Even collect strikes an important note as the season of Lent draws to a close: that passage to "our joyful resurrection" will not be because of any meritorious works we have done, but "for his merits, who died and was buried and rose again for us." This is the good news of Jesus Christ for all people (1 Corinthians 15:3-4).

Death does not have the last word. Next comes Easter Day, the memorial of our Lord's resurrection and victory over death. The gospel is John 20:1-10, recounting the discovery first by Mary Magdalene, and then by Peter and John, of the empty tomb. The other readings provide more angles from which to see the resurrection: the Passover and deliverance in the Red Sea (Exodus 12 and 14); the connection between Jesus' death and resurrection and our own death and resurrection with him in the sacrament of baptism (Romans 6); and the implications of the resurrection for how we live (Colossians 3:1-7). The last reading at Evening Prayer is a passage from the apostle Peter's sermon at Pentecost (Acts 2:22-47). Peter invokes Old Testament prophecy and draws together our Lord's crucifixion, resurrection, and ascension, making all these great fulfillments the foundation of the church's life.

Many people think that Easter ends on Easter Day. But the next two days are called the Monday and Tuesday in Easter Week, or "Easter Monday" and "Easter Tuesday." Observing days after Easter is an ancient custom that goes back to at least the time of Saint Augustine and Saint Chrysostom (around AD 400).

But antiquity is not enough for the Book of Common Prayer. Ancient customs are retained only if they're useful (see pp. 17-21). Observing Easter Monday and Tuesday allows the themes of Easter Day to continue. The gospel readings from Luke extend the story of the disciples' own "passover" from doubt to faith, from perplexity to understanding, and from sorrow to joy, as they grasp the reality of Christ's resurrection and its centrality to God's plan of salvation foretold by the prophets. The epistle readings from Acts tell how this "passover" was extended to the world by the apostolic preaching of the resurrection. At Morning and Evening Prayer on Easter Monday and Tuesday we stay in step with the story of Israel, remembering that the people were fed in the wilderness, supplied with water, and given the gift of the law (Exodus 16, 17, and 20). Yet they were still tempted to turn from their Redeemer to an idol (Exodus 32). Meanwhile the New Testament readings include our Lord's great commission (Matthew 28) and Saint Paul's exuberant meditation on the resurrection (1 Corinthians 15). Easter Monday and Tuesday once served a very practical need as well: all in the parish were expected to "make their communion" at Easter, and not everyone could be accommodated within services on Easter Day.

Next are the five Sundays after Easter, a period sometimes called "Eastertide." During this time, the epistles are taken from the "general epistles"—which is the name for the epistles of Peter, James, John, and Jude. These selections draw out implications of Jesus' death and resurrection for what we believe and do. The Sunday first lessons from the Old Testament continue Israel's movement toward the Promised Land. Just as in the ancient world a new king would declare his laws, so our newly risen king gives us his law in the readings from Deuteronomy, and the gospel readings in Eastertide anticipate the feast of the Ascension.

The Fifth Sunday after Easter, also called Rogation Sunday (p. xxiv), is followed by three days of fasting and prayer. These are called the Rogation Days (p. xxv), from the Latin word *rogare*, which means "ask." This hiatus from Eastertide feasting began in Gaul in the 400s and quickly spread to England and eventually to the rest of Europe. Traditionally it was a time to ask God's blessing on the harvest and acknowledge his gracious bounty toward sinners. But the official homily for Rogationtide bids us to recognize God's bounty in more than crops. "All good things," it tells us, "come of God, of what name and nature soever they be," not only of "corruptible things . . . but much more of all spiritual graces" fitting "for our soul."[7] The Litany is particularly appropriate for Rogationtide, and the appendix of additional prayers and thanksgivings has several other useful prayers (pp. 670, 715, 718).

Forty days after Easter comes Ascension Day. Most Christians know that Christmas and Easter are important, but Ascension isn't nearly as well-known as it should be. It is just as vital to the gospel as our Lord's birth and resurrection. When the apostle Peter proclaimed the good news on Pentecost, he describes the goal of the incarnation as the ascension and reign of Christ (Acts 2:29-32). It is affirmed in all the creeds, is pleaded in the Litany, and is the subject of one of the Articles (Article 4, p. 629).

The Book of Common Prayer follows an old English custom, going back to at least the time of King Alfred (reigned 871–899), of calling Ascension Day "Holy Thursday" (p. xxv). Ascension Day is one of only six days that have special psalms (p. xxxiii); these psalms predict the triumphant ascent of the great king. The epistle and gospel for Ascension Day tell the story of Jesus' ascension to reign at the right hand of the Father, while the epistle and gospel for the Sunday after Ascension Day emphasize the gifts the ascendant king gives to the church, especially anticipating the gift of the Holy Spirit.

The gift of the Holy Spirit is celebrated on the next Sunday, Pentecost, or as it is known in the prayer book, Whitsunday. The name probably comes from the use of this Sunday for baptisms, with the people being baptized wearing white robes, which made it white, or whit, Sunday.

On this day we remember what happened on the feast of Pentecost in the second chapter of Acts, when the Holy Spirit came upon the apostles, filling them with power to proclaim the good news of Jesus to all nations. Whitsunday has a special "preface" read by the priest in the Communion service. It begins by recounting the events of Pentecost, and then turns to why the risen and reigning Lord gave this most divine gift to the apostles: "To teach them and to lead them to all truth, giving them both the gift of divers languages and also boldness with fervent zeal constantly to preach the gospel unto all nations, whereby we have been brought out of darkness and error into the clear light and true knowledge of thee and of thy Son Jesus Christ" (p. 260).

Just like Easter, Whitsunday keeps going for two more days. Monday and Tuesday in Whitsun Week have readings that illuminate the Holy Spirit's work. For example, the first lesson for Morning Prayer on Monday is Genesis 11:1-9, and with that choice the Book of Common Prayer presents Pentecost as a reversal of Babel: there the people were divided into many languages; here they are all brought together to hear the good news of Jesus Christ. As Saint Augustine put it, although

> the human race was deservedly divided by languages, so that each nation would speak its own language and thus not be understood by the others; so in a similar way the devout humility of the faithful has brought to the unity of the Church the variety of their different languages; so that what discord had dissipated charity might gather together, and the scattered members of the human race, as of one body, might be attached to their one head, Christ, and so reunited, and fused together into the unity of the holy body by the fire of love.[8]

Indeed, love is a major theme across these three special days of Whitsunday, Whitsun Monday, and Whitsun Tuesday. The gospel on Whitsunday speaks of the love within the Trinity, and God's love for us, and our love for God shown by keeping his commandments (John 14:15-31). The gospel on the Monday in Whitsun Week includes John 3:16 (which also appears in the Comfortable Words in Holy Communion, p. 258). And the Old Testament lesson for Evensong on Whitsun Tuesday is Deuteronomy 30, which says to obey, love, and turn to God "with all your heart and with all your soul" (Deuteronomy 30:2, 6, 10 RSV).

The last reading on these three days is 1 John 4:1-13, which reminds us that the Spirit of God can be counterfeited—so "test the spirits"—but it also serves as a stirring conclusion to all the incarnation feasts. In verse 9, the apostle John writes words that make us think of Advent, Christmas, and Epiphany: "In this was manifested the love of God toward us, because that God sent his only begotten Son into the world, that we might live through him." Verse 10 continues with words that make us think of Good Friday: "Herein is love, not that we loved God, but that he loved us, and sent his Son to be the propitiation for our sins." Verse 11 draws the lesson for how we live: "Beloved, if God so loved us, we ought also to love one another" (KJV). Like a runner in a relay race passing the baton to the next runner, these readings lead perfectly to the second half of the church year, where we begin again with love.

TRINITY: THE SECOND HALF OF THE CHURCH YEAR

The second half of the church year takes its name from its first Sunday. Trinity Sunday is one of the last developments in the church calendar that is included in the Book of Common Prayer. The observance of Trinity Sunday spread in the 900s, and it was popular in England, France, Germany, and the Low Countries, but it was not observed universally in the West until the 1300s. This feast was retained at the Reformation because it expresses the catholic teaching on the Trinity. Trinity Sunday is especially fitting after the feasts of the incarnation, because those feasts tend to emphasize the distinction among the persons of the Trinity, while this Sunday emphasizes the unity.

On this day, the readings for Morning and Evening Prayer include Old Testament allusions to the Trinity (Genesis 1 and 18), explicit New Testament teaching about the Trinity (Matthew 3), and the implications of the Trinity's work for how we live (1 John 5). The Athanasian Creed is said at Morning Prayer, and since it was also said on Ascension Day and Whitsunday, this is the peak Athanasian Creed time in the entire year.

The Communion readings for Trinity Sunday are older than the observance of Trinity Sunday itself. Because they were originally for the Sunday following Pentecost, there is an emphasis on the Holy Spirit. But in these readings the Spirit points us to the Son, which makes them a perfect way to move from Whitsunday to Trinity Sunday. Revelation 4, the reading appointed for the epistle on Trinity Sunday, offers an awe-inspiring vision of heaven, as Saint John is "in the Spirit" and sees the incarnate Son of God seated on the divine throne and acclaimed as Lord. The gospel, John 3:1-15, describes the work of the Holy Spirit and the Son of God. Thus the epistle and gospel speak of the outward work of the Trinity—of our entrance into the kingdom of God (eternal life) by the redemptive work of his Son and the regenerating work of his Spirit. As with the lessons for Morning and Evening Prayer, these readings teach us about the Trinity through narratives. There's an old maxim about good writing: "Show, don't tell." That's what these readings do: we learn what the Trinity is by seeing what the Trinity does.

The Sundays after Trinity are sometimes called "Trinitytide." In medieval England, as well as other parts of northern Europe, the Sundays in this part of the year were numbered after Trinity Sunday: the First Sunday after Trinity, the Second Sunday after Trinity, and so on. In other places, including France, the Sundays in this part of the year were numbered after Pentecost: the First Sunday after Pentecost, and so on. Rome eventually settled on numbering the Sundays after Pentecost, while Anglicans and Lutherans continued to number the Sundays after Trinity.

In the Trinity half of the year, the prayers and readings shift the emphasis. The incarnation half emphasized redemption, what God has done *for* us. Now, Trinitytide turns us toward sanctification, what God is doing *in* us. In the first half of the church year, we had the high mountains of Christmas and Easter and the deep valleys of Ash Wednesday and Good Friday. But in the Trinity season, we have a level path, a steady course.

You might have heard the term "ordinary time" before, as an idea for any miscellaneous time that doesn't fit in the seasons of Advent, Christmas, Lent, and Easter. That term is surprisingly new, dating only back to 1970 in the Roman Catholic Church. By contrast, almost all of the aspects of the church year in the Book of Common Prayer are much older, usually one thousand to fifteen hundred years old. So the prayer book doesn't have "ordinary time." It treats Epiphanytide, the 'Gesimas, and the Sundays after Trinity as distinct seasons, each with its own character and emphasis.

During the first half of the year, the gospel readings tend to strike the keynote. They are describing these great events of our salvation, and the epistles are the supporting cast. But when we get to the Trinity season, the epistles tend to be central. There's a little bit of history that explains this. There was a list of epistle readings for Sundays used in Rome as early as the 600s. We do not have the exact list, and it was modified some over time as it spread through the Western church. But the basic pattern was to read selections from the general epistles on ten Sundays after Easter, and then to read selections from the Pauline epistles, working through them in the order in which they're in the Bible. That sequence appears in the Book of Common Prayer. Beginning on the First Sunday after Easter and continuing through the Third Sunday after Trinity, the epistles are taken from the general epistles. Then we get a greatest-hits collection from the epistles of Saint Paul in biblical order (Trinity 6 through Trinity 24).

The themes for the epistles in Trinitytide are listed below, but note how they begin: with an emphasis on love. In the Book of Common Prayer, every season begins by emphasizing God's love to us or our love to God and neighbor. Advent begins with "Owe no man anything, but to love one another" (p. 49). On the Sunday before the beginning of

Lent, the epistle is 1 Corinthians 13, the great chapter on charity (p. 85). The Sunday next before Easter emphasizes God's "tender love towards mankind" (p. 100).

SUNDAYS AFTER TRINITY: THE EPISTLES

1st:	1 John 4:7-21	(we love God, because he first loved us)
2nd:	1 John 3:13-24	(because God loves us, love one another)
3rd:	1 Peter 5:5-11	(humility amid suffering)
4th:	Romans 8:18-23	(hope amid suffering)
5th:	1 Peter 3:8-15	(peace amid persecution)
6th:	Romans 6:3-11	(baptized with Jesus, we are dead to sin)
7th:	Romans 6:19-23	(serving sin leads to death, but we are servants of God)
8th:	Romans 8:12-17	(living after the flesh leads to death, but we are sons of God)
9th:	1 Corinthians 10:1-13	(spiritual privileges are not enough)
10th:	1 Corinthians 12:1-11	(many gifts but one Spirit)
11th:	1 Corinthians 15:1-11	(our salvation depends on the resurrection)
12th:	2 Corinthians 3:4-9	(the superiority of the new covenant over the law)
13th:	Galatians 3:16-22	(the superiority of the promise over the law)
14th:	Galatians 5:16-24	(works of the flesh contrasted with fruit of the Spirit)
15th:	Galatians 6:11-18	(glory not in your flesh, but only in the cross)

16th: Ephesians 3:13-21   (the Trinity enables you to
                                know the love of Christ)

17th: Ephesians 4:1-6   (bear with one another in love
                                because there is one body and
                                one Spirit)

18th: 1 Corinthians 1:4-8   (the gifts of God are given to
                                make us blameless at the
                                coming of the Lord)

19th: Ephesians 4:17-32   (put on the new man and do
                                not grieve the Spirit who seals
                                us for the day of redemption)

20th: Ephesians 5:15-21   (the days are evil, so walk
                                wisely)

21st: Ephesians 6:10-20   (take the whole armor of God
                                to withstand in the evil day)

22nd: Philippians 1:3-11   (pray with confidence that God
                                will perform his work in us
                                until the day of Jesus Christ)

23rd: Philippians 3:17-21   (as citizens of heaven, look for
                                our coming Savior, who will
                                change our bodies to be like his)

24th: Colossians 1:3-12   (pray with thanksgiving, for
                                the work of God to continue
                                in us)

25th: Jeremiah 23:5-8   (the Lord Our Righteousness is
                                coming to deliver his people)
                                This is always used on the last
                                Sunday before Advent.

The readings from the Pauline epistles follow the biblical order, with the exception of the epistle for the Eighteenth Sunday after Trinity. The reason, perhaps, is that Trinity 18 sometimes coincided with a time for the ordination of new ministers. The Trinity 18 epistle is especially suited to that purpose.

At the beginning of Trinitytide, the theme is love, or charity, which connects with Whitsunday. After that, although there is not a single unifying theme, there are connections from week to week, with a recurring emphasis on suffering; on baptism; on withstanding the world, the flesh, and the devil; on the new covenant; and on the gifts and fruit of the Spirit. At point after point in this ancient pattern, preserved in the Book of Common Prayer, the gospel seems to be chosen to complement the epistle.

As Trinitytide draws to a close, around the Eighteenth Sunday after Trinity, the epistles begin to strike a note of eschatological anticipation. They start to direct our attention to thinking about the Second Coming of our Lord. In addition, the epistle for the Twenty-First Sunday after Trinity is concerned with the Christian's armor—a topic that readies us for the First Sunday in Advent, with its collect asking for God to "put upon us the armour of light" (p. 49).

Trinitytide also leads perfectly into Advent for another reason. In the Sundays after Trinity, we are learning about godly living, and as we do, we will inevitably be aware not only of our duties but also of our shortcomings. That leads us to think of the judgment to come, and the importance of being found in Christ at his Second Coming (2 Peter 3:14; Philippians 3:9). And that is how the season of Advent begins.

One of the earliest commentators on the Book of Common Prayer was Anthony Sparrow. He published his commentary anonymously in 1655, when Oliver Cromwell was Lord

Protector and it was illegal to use the prayer book in church. In fact, Sparrow himself had been forced out of his church several years earlier for using the prayer book in services. Sparrow, who would later become a bishop, wrote that in the first half of the church year we celebrate "the high festivals" and "mysteries of our redemption by Christ on earth." These feasts take us "through a great part of the creed," culminating in Whitsunday. That movement tracks the Apostles' Creed, where the last section begins with "I believe in the Holy Ghost." But in the second half of the year, the church has given us readings that "tend to our edifying, and being the living temples of the Holy Ghost our Comforter, with his gifts and graces, that having oil in our lamps, we may be in better readiness to meet the Bridegroom at his second advent or coming to judgment"[9] (compare Matthew 25:1-13).

Thus the Trinity season carries us from Pentecost to Advent, which prepares us for another yearly cycle. Truly, as the apostle Peter said, we need to recall what we already know (2 Peter 1:12).

9

The Communion of Saints

✝

Just over sixteen centuries ago, in a small city in North Africa, the bishop stood up and began his sermon: "The gospel that has just been read about Christ the Lord, and how he walked over the surface of the sea, and about the apostle Peter, and how, by growing afraid as he walked, he staggered, and by losing confidence began to submerge, until by confessing he again emerged; this gospel is advising us to take the sea as meaning the present age and this world, and the apostle Peter as representing the one and only Church."[1]

After recalling many New Testament passages about Peter, the bishop said:

> Notice that man Peter, who was the symbolic representative of us all: now he's trusting, now he's tottering;

one moment he's acknowledging Christ to be immortal, the next he's afraid of his dying. It's because the Church of Christ in the same sort of way has strong members, and also has weak members. It can't do without its strong members, nor without its weak ones. That's why the apostle Paul says, *But we who are strong should bear the burdens of the weak* (Rom 15:1). Now Peter, in saying *You are the Christ, the Son of the living God* (Mt 16:16), represents the strong. But in his being filled with alarm, and his staggering, and not wanting Christ to suffer because he was afraid of death and didn't recognize life, he represents the weak members of the Church. . . . Without the one or the other there is no Church.[2]

The bishop who preached that sermon about Saint Peter as a figure of the church was Saint Augustine of Hippo. His description of Saint Peter can help us think about what it means to call someone a saint.

The word *saint* is used in the Book of Common Prayer in two senses. First, it's a term for Christians generally. That's how it's used in the epistles and gospels (for example, Ephesians 5:3 KJV). *Saints* also has a broad sense in the prayer book translation of the Psalms (for example, Psalm 132:9).

Second, *saint* can be a title of honor. It is used for the biblical apostles and writers of the gospels (called "evangelists"), and for other Christians who are exemplary in reflecting the character and virtues of Jesus Christ. This is what *saint* means in the calendar, the collects, and the Articles. We find repeated references, for example, to both "Saint Peter the Apostle" (pp. xxv, xxxii, xliv, 225, 292, 322, 659, 684, 746) and "Saint Augustine" (pp. xix, xlviii, 640, 660).

Those two senses are tied together: Saint Peter and Saint Augustine, one from Asia and one from Africa, are examples of holiness for all Christians. The saints in the narrow sense, even though fallible and sometimes fearful, are trail-blazers, runners who have finished the race (Hebrews 12:2). So in the Communion service, we bless God for the saints, who are his servants, and ask that he would "give us grace so to follow their good examples, that with them we may be partakers of thy heavenly kingdom" (p. 251). We honor the saints as servants of God, who as servants would not take any worship or veneration that belongs to God alone (Acts 14:14-15). As one of the official homilies puts it, the saints "were the true servants of God, and did give all honour to him, taking none unto themselves, and are blessed souls with God."[3]

The lives of the saints therefore are vivid pictures of the body of Christ and the work of the Holy Spirit. A Lutheran theologian said it well: "The lives of the saints . . . [are] a reminder of the continuing existence of the body of Christ—the Church—and of the fact that whether it be militant and on earth or triumphant and in heaven, it is one, holy, catholic church, timeless and composed of God's people in every age."[4]

THE SAINTS AND THE REFORMATION

In the late Middle Ages, the Church had a calendar chock-full of saints. By and large, the leading English reformers did not want to eradicate these examples of holiness from the church calendar, yet they had serious concerns to address.

One concern was the legendary or historically dubious saints. Take for example Saint Tiburtius. Nothing is known about him except, maybe, where he's buried. Or Saint Thecla. Many legends were invented about her in the apocryphal "Acts of Saints Paul and Thecla," but we aren't sure she ever existed. Given her dubious authenticity, she was removed from the calendar of the Roman Catholic Church in the 1960s.

A second concern was complexity. The system of devotion and commemoration of the saints was developed for monks and nuns, and it was too complicated and overwhelming for the laity. But the laity were exactly who the English reformers wanted to know the gospel. All the people should hear the word of God and participate in the work of prayer.

A third concern was doctrine. The commemoration of saints was often tied to praying *to* saints, as well as the idea that the merits of the saints were available to shave a few years off time in purgatory. The English reformers wanted the commemoration of the saints not to distract from the gospel, but to be an occasion for presenting the gospel. The saints, too, were saved only by grace. They cannot give us more effective access to God or postmortem advantages (Article 22, p. 637; also Article 14, p. 633).

A related doctrinal question concerned Marian devotion. The English reformers held the Blessed Virgin Mary, the mother of Jesus, in very high esteem. Several feasts in the prayer book—especially Christmas, the Presentation, and the Annunciation—recognize the faith and obedience of the Virgin from whom the eternal Son assumed flesh for our redemption. These feasts can be traced back to the first centuries of the church, but when they began, their primary focus was on our Lord, not on his mother. As the centuries wore on, that focus often shifted to the Virgin Mary and to beliefs about her that lack a basis in Scripture, with more and more days added to the calendar to commemorate her. The English reformers knew that the Virgin Mary always pointed others beyond herself to her Son (for example, John 2:5), and they wanted that to be reflected in how she is commemorated in the calendar.

In short, the calendar of saints' days had much that was good, but it needed to be reformed. The result was a greatly streamlined list of saints' days in the first Book of Common Prayer (1549), which was further revised in each new edition of the prayer book (1552, 1559, 1604, 1662).

A Sketch of the Saints' Days

The calendar in the Book of Common Prayer commemorates certain saints with "red-letter days," so called because they are marked in red in the calendar that starts on page xxxiv. (In some editions they are distinguished with italics instead of red letters.) On other days, called "black-letter days," the names of people and events in the calendar are printed in black. The black-letter days are discussed at the end of this chapter.

There are twenty-one red-letter saints' days. They commemorate biblical saints or events, with the exception of All

Saints' Day (November 1), which condenses the commemoration of all other saints down to a single day. Most of the red-letter saints' days commemorate the apostles and evangelists. There are also commemorations of Saint Stephen, who was the first martyr, and of Saint Michael and All Angels. And there are commemorations of five events: Herod's slaughter of the innocents, Saint Paul's conversion, the presentation of Christ in the temple, the Annunciation, and the birth of John the Baptist.

For each red-letter saint's day there is a collect that is "proper" to the day, usually one newly written by Archbishop Cranmer. It typically mentions a theme from the life of the saint, and then pivots to asking God for something we need that is basic to the Christian life. The collect often ties the saint's day to the season in the church year.

There are also special readings for the red-letter saints' days. For Morning and Evening Prayer, the proper first lessons are usually from Job, Proverbs, and Ecclesiastes, or else from the books of the Apocrypha, such as Sirach or the Wisdom of Solomon. Collectively these books from the Old Testament and Apocrypha are called "Wisdom literature," and they are read because we look to the saints as examples of true wisdom (James 3:13-18). Each red-letter day also has a proper epistle and gospel for a service of Holy Communion or Ante-Communion after Morning Prayer. As with the other feast days described in chapter eight, the expectation is that there will be services of Communion or Ante-Communion in church on these days.

THROUGH THE YEAR WITH
THE RED-LETTER SAINTS' DAYS

Here are the red-letter saints' days, listed in the order of the church year (pp. 205-40):

November 30: Saint Andrew's Day. Saint Andrew was a disciple of Jesus and the brother of Peter, and according to an early Christian tradition he was a missionary and a martyr by crucifixion. The gospel of the day recounts how Jesus called Andrew and Peter, and "they straightway left their nets and followed him." That obedience is the theme of the collect. But how are we supposed to imitate the example of Saint Andrew? We won't be fishing in the Sea of Galilee while Jesus happens to walk by on the beach and speak to us. But as we read the Scriptures, we will hear the call of God and decide how to respond. The collect asks that God would give us grace to obey that word: "Grant unto us all, that we, being called by thy holy word, may forthwith give up ourselves obediently to fulfil thy holy commandments." The collect underscores that this calling is not just for the clergy or really advanced Christians—"Grant unto us all."

December 21: Saint Thomas the Apostle. Thomas is another of Jesus' first disciples, famous as "Doubting Thomas." He refused to believe the resurrection unless he could touch where the spear pierced Jesus' side and where the nails were driven into his hands. But when Thomas saw Jesus, and was told to touch his hands and side, he exclaimed, "My Lord, and my God!" The collect asks that God, who allowed Thomas to doubt the resurrection, would grant us to "without all doubt believe in thy Son Jesus Christ." The epistle connects the confession of Thomas to the founding of the church, which is "built upon the foundation of the apostles and prophets, Jesus Christ himself being the chief cornerstone." According to one ancient tradition, Saint Thomas carried the gospel to India.

The feast of Saint Thomas falls in Advent, ensuring that we start the church year with the challenge of faith: do we believe in Jesus Christ? It is the shortest, darkest day of the year, just a few days before Christmas—a reminder that it is not in us to believe, but it is the gift of Jesus Christ, the light of the world.

December 26: Saint Stephen's Day; December 27: Saint John the Evangelist's Day; December 28: The Innocents' Day. If you look for the next red-letter saint's day, you will think it's the Conversion of Saint Paul (p. 208). But there are red-letter days on December 26, 27, and 28. The prayer book puts their materials right after Christmas Day (pp. 59-64). These days continue the celebration of Christmas, just like Easter Monday and Tuesday continue the themes of Easter.

But you might be surprised when you look at what these days are about. Saint Stephen was the first martyr, stoned to death for his witness to Jesus. Saint John wrote in exile. The Innocents' Day remembers King Herod's slaughter of the young boys when he was trying to kill Jesus. Isn't this Christmas? Why are we turning our eyes to these horrors?

On Christmas Day, we see the baby Jesus through the eyes of his mother, the Virgin Mary (Isaiah 7:14; Luke 2:7). But on these three days we see Jesus from other vantage points.

On Saint Stephen's Day, we see Jesus with the eyes of the first martyr of the New Testament church, a man in the prime of life, who had just delivered a powerful sermon that stirred the hatred of his hearers. Stephen "looked up steadfastly into heaven, and saw the glory of God and Jesus standing on the right hand of God" (Acts 7:55 KJV). In the 400s, theologian Fulgentius of Ruspe wrote, "The love that brought Christ down from heaven to earth raised Stephen from earth to heaven. . . . His love of God kept him from yielding to the ferocious mob; his love for his neighbour made him pray for those who were stoning him. Love inspired him to reprove those who erred, to make them amend; love led him to pray for those who stoned him, to save them from punishment."[5]

On Saint John the Evangelist's Day, we see Jesus with the eyes of an old man, about ninety years old, living in exile on the island of Patmos, beholding the visions of the Apocalypse. The Apocalypse, also called the Book of Revelation, provides the New Testament readings for Morning and Evening Prayer on this feast day. These readings echo ones from the previous day for Saint Stephen: both saints saw their visions by the power of the Holy Spirit (Acts 7:55; Revelation 1:10), and both beheld Jesus as "the Son of Man" foreseen by Daniel (Acts 7:56; Revelation 1:13). The epistle for Saint John the Evangelist's Day bears witness to the purpose of the incarnation: "That ye might have fellowship with us, and truly our fellowship is with the Father, and with his Son Jesus Christ."

On the Innocents' Day, we see Jesus with the eyes of infant children, young boys, victims of the blind fury of King Herod. They were killed not because of anything they had done, but because Herod sought to kill a rival. The gospel tells of Rachel "weeping for her children, and would not be comforted, because they are not" (Matthew 2:18 KJV). In the weeping of these devastated mothers, grieving the loss of their sons, we see what would come for the Virgin Mary. Yet the reading for the epistle lets us see further. Just as Saint Stephen and Saint John looked into heaven, so we are taken into heaven and see "a Lamb," who "stood on the Mount Sion," and with him are 144,000 saints, the redeemed, who "follow the Lamb" and have "his Father's name written in their foreheads." They stand "without fault before the throne of God." With the church's choice of this reading, we are called to think of these youngest of martyrs, the innocents, as always with the Lord for whom they suffered. It is striking that one of the psalms always read on the Innocents' Day is Psalm 139; this psalm describes how God loved and fashioned each one of these children from the womb.

So these three days offer us three pictures side by side, a triptych about the incarnation of Jesus Christ and what it means for us. Each picture depicts one of the three ages of man (a popular theme in Renaissance art). All three show us bitter suffering. They confront us with the extremities of martyrdom, from an infant's death to an elder's exile. These days teach us that the birth of Jesus does not transport us out of this life in which suffering and spiritual warfare are constant companions.

Yet all three days startle us out of our material and earthly surroundings, prompting us to catch a heavenly vision. What is the incarnation for? Where is it headed? What will happen to death? In the readings for these days, we have the answers. We see and hear our Lord, who says, "I . . . have the keys of hell and of death" (Revelation 1:18 KJV, read at Morning Prayer on Saint John's Day). With the eyes of faith we look from this beginning, the babe in the manger, to the final consummation of all things: "And there shall be no more curse: but the throne of God and of the Lamb shall be in it; and his servants shall serve him: And they shall see his face; and his name shall be on their foreheads. And there shall be no night there; and they need no candle, neither light of the sun; for the Lord God giveth them light: and they shall reign for ever and ever" (Revelation 22:3-5 KJV, read at Evening Prayer on Saint John's Day).

January 25: The Conversion of Saint Paul. It is fitting that the feast of "the apostle to the Gentiles" falls in Epiphanytide, which celebrates the manifestation of Christ to the Gentiles. The Epiphany theme of light is continued in the collect: "O God, who, through the preaching of the blessed apostle Saint Paul, hast caused the light of the gospel to shine throughout the world." The collect asks for grace to respond with thankfulness to the gospel by following "the holy doctrine" that Saint Paul taught. Note that Paul persecuted Stephen, so in these two days, almost a month apart, we see how Jesus Christ can transform a heart.[6]

February 24: Saint Matthias's Day. Saint Matthias was the apostle chosen to replace Judas (Acts 1:15-26). His day falls during Lent or the pre-Lent season of Gesimatide, and the collect looks ahead to the days before Easter, and specifically to the betrayal of Christ. It begins: "O almighty God, who into the place of the traitor Judas didst choose thy faithful servant Matthias to be of the number of the twelve apostles." This collect is one of several that underscore the need for faithful leadership in the church. It asks God to grant that the church would be "alway preserved from false apostles" and "be ordered and guided by faithful and true pastors." In the gospel, Jesus thanks the Father who has "kept these things"—the truths of the kingdom—"from the wise and prudent, and hast revealed them unto babes." Not in the pride of intellect, but only in the humility of faith, can we know the Father, through the one who is "meek and lowly in heart."

March 25: The Annunciation of the Blessed Virgin Mary. *Annunciation* means "announcement," and this day commemorates the announcement to the Blessed Virgin Mary that she would bear the Messiah. It is exactly nine months before Christmas Day. This collect puts us into the story in Luke 1, as we stand beside the Virgin Mary and hear of "the incarnation . . . by the message of an angel." The feast of the Annunciation usually falls near the end of Lent, sometimes even falling on Good Friday—as in 1608, when the pastor-poet John Donne described the juxtaposition as "this doubtful day / Of feast or fast, Christ came, and went away."[7] The collect makes this day a hinge, turning back to remember Christmas and turning forward to anticipate Good

Friday and Easter Day, asking that "by his cross and passion we may be brought unto the glory of his resurrection."

April 25: Saint Mark's Day. Saint Mark is one of the four evangelists, and the New Testament records that he assisted Saint Paul in his missionary work, before deserting him and later returning again. Saint Mark's Day almost always falls during Eastertide. We have just celebrated central events of the gospel—from the passion of our Lord to his resurrection—and the collect asks that God would keep us from being "like children carried away with every blast of vain doctrine," and instead would make us "established in the truth" of the "holy gospel." The gospel of the day belongs to the Eastertide readings drawn from the Last Supper discourses. Only as we abide in Christ, as branches abide in the vine, can we bring forth fruit, "for apart from me ye can do nothing." Saint Mark's Gospel drives home this doctrine with its unsparing honesty about the failures of the disciples when they relied on themselves. The epistle points to the only source of fruitful ministry: the gifts the ascended Lord bestows on the church.

May 1: Saint Philip and Saint James's Day. On this day two saints are commemorated. One is Saint Philip, who in the gospel of the day fails to understand what Jesus is teaching or doing, asking "Show us the Father," right after Jesus has just said, "I am the way, the truth, and the life." The collect is built on the way-truth-life triad—variations on these words appear seven times!

The other saint commemorated on this day is Saint James. But *James* is the name of at least two or three people in the

New Testament. One is the son of Zebedee and brother of Saint John, James the Great, commemorated on July 25. The Saint James commemorated today with Saint Philip is James the son of Alphaeus (Matthew 10:3), also known as James the Less. He is sometimes identified with the Lord's brother, James the Just, traditionally considered the first bishop of the church in Jerusalem (Acts 15:13; Galatians 1:19), and the epistle of the day is taken from his epistle.

June 11: Saint Barnabas the Apostle. Barnabas's name means "son of consolation" and the record of his ministry in Acts indicates that providing encouragement and comfort was his special gift. Barnabas accompanied the apostle Paul on some of his missionary journeys, and though he was not one of the twelve apostles, he is described as an apostle in Acts 14:14. In the reading for the epistle, Barnabas is called "a good man, and full of the Holy Ghost and of faith." The collect picks up on the idea of being filled with the Holy Spirit, and it asks God—who filled the apostle Barnabas with "singular gifts"—to fill us, the whole church, with the Spirit's "manifold gifts." This emphasis on the Holy Spirit is perfectly timed, for Saint Barnabas is almost always the first red-letter saint's day after Pentecost.

June 24: Saint John the Baptist's Day. Another name for this day is "The Nativity of Saint John the Baptist" (p. xxv), and its timing is derived from the Annunciation (March 25). When the angel Gabriel announced to the Blessed Virgin Mary that she would bear a son, he said that her cousin Elizabeth—the mother of John the Baptist—was "now in her sixth month" (Luke 1:36 REB). Three months later is

June 24. The epistle and gospel, as well as the proper lessons from Malachi and Matthew, have us look past John the Baptist to see the Greater One for whom he prepared the way.

June 29: Saint Peter's Day. This feast began in Rome in AD 258 during the persecution of the church by the Emperor Valerian (reigned AD 253-260). Originally it was a feast for the martyrdom of both Saint Peter and Saint Paul, who were also celebrated individually on other days. When Archbishop Cranmer set out to simplify the church calendar, he left one day to commemorate each of these saints: the Conversion of Saint Paul on January 25 and Saint Peter's Day on June 29. Cranmer composed a collect that draws together language from a number of passages of Scripture, highlighting the reciprocal duties of pastor and flock, of shepherds and sheep. The epistle describes the first state-sponsored persecution of Christians, while the gospel recounts Peter's confession. The correspondence is striking: the first disciple to confess that Jesus is the Christ is the first person to be put in chains for that faith.

July 25: Saint James the Apostle. Saint James was one of Jesus' apostles, the brother of John, and the only apostle whose martyrdom is noted in the New Testament. The epistle of the day was selected by Archbishop Cranmer because it contains the verse from Acts referring to Saint James's martyrdom. For the gospel, the medieval service books had Matthew 20:20-23, which is fitting because our Lord foretells that martyrdom. But Cranmer was alert for spiritual lessons for all Christians, even those who might not face martyrdom like Saint James (or, as it turned out, like

Cranmer himself). So Cranmer lengthened the gospel for the feast of Saint James, adding five verses (Matthew 20:24-28) that describe true greatness in the kingdom of God—not wielding dominion, but serving.

August 24: Saint Bartholomew the Apostle. Saint Bartholomew is identified as one of the twelve disciples in the Gospels of Matthew, Mark, and Luke, and he is sometimes thought to be the same person as Nathaniel in the Gospel of John. According to one tradition, he preached the gospel in "India" (which might refer to modern-day Arabia or Ethiopia), and his feast day was first celebrated by the Eastern churches. The collect asks that the church would "love that word that he believed" and also "preach and receive the same." This is a nice example of how the collects reinforce the responsibilities of both the clergy and laity: if the duty of preaching is for ministers, the duties of loving and receiving the word of God are for everyone. Both the epistle and the gospel point us toward humble service. The reading for the epistle recounts how the apostles ministered to the sick, needy, and weak, while the gospel shows they were following the example of their Lord, exhibiting the greatness that is characteristic of his kingdom.

September 21: Saint Matthew the Apostle. Before he was a disciple of Jesus, Saint Matthew was a tax collector (a "publican"). Tax collectors were hated. They were agents of the Roman Empire and known for their greed. The gospel tells of Matthew's obedience to Jesus' call, and the collect asks that the same God who graciously called Matthew would "grant us grace to forsake all covetous desires and inordinate love of riches, and to follow the same thy Son Jesus Christ." This is the third and last of the red-letter days for which the collect holds before us an example of a disciple who heard the call of Jesus and answered. The epistle teaches how that transformation happens: "For God, who commanded the light to shine out of darkness, hath shined in our hearts, to give the light of the knowledge of the glory of God in the face of Jesus Christ."

September 29: Saint Michael and All Angels. This festival seems to date to the late 300s when a basilica was dedicated to Saint Michael a few miles outside Rome. Michael is an archangel referred to in the books of Daniel, Jude, and Revelation. The collect does not mention Michael, however. It concentrates on how God has ordered the service of both angels and mankind, and it asks that God would appoint the angels to "succour and defend us on earth." *Succour* means "to help or aid" (p. 761), and here it has a military connotation—reinforcements from the army of heaven—which fits the way angels are often described in the Scriptures (for example, 2 Kings 6:17). That emphasis on spiritual warfare appears in the reading for the epistle and the proper lessons. For the Christian, these passages call to mind the baptismal service, where the sign of the cross is applied to the baptized "in token that hereafter *he* shall not be ashamed to confess the faith of Christ crucified, and manfully to fight under his banner against sin, the world, and the devil, and to continue Christ's faithful soldier and servant unto *his* life's end" (p. 278).

But courage is not the only virtue. The gospel commends a childlike humility, the opposite or answer to the spirit of pride that animates Satan, the very reason he was cast out of heaven. The epistle, with its account of Michael casting "that proud spirit" out of heaven, is a counterpart to the teaching of the gospel of the day that greatness in the kingdom is for the humble.

October 18: Saint Luke the Evangelist. Saint Luke was a physician and the author of both the gospel that bears his name and its sequel, the Acts of the Apostles. The collect for Saint Luke's Day, composed by Archbishop Cranmer, is both beautiful and weighty. It begins by noting that Luke received a divine call to be a different kind of physician: an evangelist who cured the maladies of the soul. And his "praise," the collect says, "is in the gospel," which means that we remember him not because of his skill in physical medicine, but because he labored with the apostle Paul to take the good news of salvation to the Gentiles (Colossians 4:14; compare 2 Corinthians 8:18). These points lead to the request in the collect: that it would please God that "all the diseases of our souls may be healed." The cure is not in our own efforts—remember the line from the general confession, "And there is no health in us" (p. 3)—but it lies instead in "the wholesome medicines delivered by" Saint Luke in his writings. A daily dose of those healing medicines is given in Morning and Evening Prayer, where the *Benedictus*, *Magnificat*, and *Nunc dimittis*, all taken from Luke's Gospel, proclaim the glorious salvation that God offers through the work of the long-anticipated Messiah. Fittingly, the collect ends with a reference to that work: "Through the merits of thy Son Jesus Christ our Lord. *Amen.*"

October 28: Saint Simon and Saint Jude, Apostles. Although Saint Simon and Saint Jude were among the twelve disciples (Luke 6:15-16), nothing else is known for certain about them. According to one tradition they preached the gospel in Persia and were martyred. The collect describes the church with the metaphor of a temple under construction. God is building the church on the foundation of the apostles and prophets, with Jesus the chief cornerstone. The epistle emphasizes judgment on sin as well as God's action to deliver his people. The gospel teaches that the Triune God will be with his people, even amid persecution.

The feast of Saint Simon and Saint Jude is followed only four days later by All Saints' Day, and the propers for these two days are strikingly connected. The collect for each feast develops a metaphor for the church (temple, body). For both feasts, the gospel ends with overcoming persecution. And the epistle about judgment on Saint Simon and Saint Jude's Day is matched by an epistle about salvation on All Saints' Day.

November 1: All Saints' Day. "It is in every way appropriate that the series of holy days, on which we commemorate particular saints, should be closed, and as it were crowned, by one comprehensive commemoration of *all* God's 'servants departed this life in his faith and fear,' and whose names are written in the book of life, however completely they may have dropped out of the memory of man."[8] The collect reminds us of the two different senses of *saint*. The broad sense of all Christians is here: Christ's "mystical body," "the elect" (compare Article 17, pp. 634-5). And so

156

is the narrow sense: the "blessed saints" whose example we follow. This collect also starts to point us toward Advent, which turns our attention toward the incarnation of our Lord Jesus Christ, as we say the saints are "knit together . . . in one communion and fellowship, in the mystical body of thy Son Christ our Lord."

The reading for the epistle is taken from Revelation, which brings us back to thinking of the feasts immediately following Christmas—Saint Stephen's Day, Saint John the Evangelist, and the Innocents' Day—because we again catch a glimpse of the Son of God in heaven with the saints gathered around the divine throne. The epistle ends dramatically and liturgically, as the saints in heaven ascribe all praise and worship to God, and from our hearts resounds the "Amen."

The gospel for All Saints' Day, the Beatitudes, ends with the blessedness of those who are persecuted. The first saints to be commemorated were martyrs, honored because of their total identification with Christ in death. This principle was later extended by the church to "confessors"—those who endured persecution, and sometimes torture, but were not martyred. That principle was gradually extended to more saints who persevered in running the race, holding on to the faith whose author and finisher is Jesus Christ (Hebrews 12:1-2). But the saints whose example we follow are not utterly unlike us. For we are all "knit together," as the collect puts it, into "one communion and fellowship." Their course is the same as ours. They are simply up the road ahead of us, having already reached the "unspeakable joys" prepared by God for all those who "unfeignedly love" him.

THE BLACK-LETTER SAINTS' DAYS

Many other saints are mentioned in the prayer book calendar, but their names are printed in black. On these black-letter days, nothing changes in the liturgy—there are no special prayers or readings. Which means you might wonder why they are there. It seems they were kept in the calendar for two reasons.

One is that they were needed for civic life. For example, schools would start their "Hilary Term" on Saint Hilary's day (January 13), so it needed to be in the calendar. And contracts were made where one side promised to pay another "on Saint Martin's Day" (November 11). On black-letter days, fairs and guild-feasts were held, and parish anniversaries were commemorated. For the black-letter days with obscure names, you can find help in the glossary in the 1662 International Edition.

The other reason for retaining the black-letter days is that they remind us of "the great cloud of witnesses" who have gone before us (Hebrews 12:1). God's work in the church did not end with the apostles and evangelists. Saint Paul ran with endurance the same race that was run by a Jewish woman (Mary Magdalene, July 22) and a Roman girl (Agnes, January 21), the same race that was run by an archbishop from Africa (Cyprian, September 26) and an archbishop from Wales (David, March 1). It is the same race that all the saints—all those whom God has set apart in Christ—continue to run today.

The black-letter days were revised in each new edition of the prayer book. Of the ones in the 1662 calendar, almost all had been observed in late medieval England, along with very many others not added back in. There are two exceptions to this rule that the black-letter days in the 1662 calendar were observed in medieval England.

One exception is a name added in 1604. Queen Elizabeth I, who reigned for more than four decades, had recently died and been succeeded by her cousin King James VI of Scotland (who became King James I of England). The Queen's birthday, September 7, had been noted in the calendar, but with the accession of James, her birthday would be deleted and the new king's birthday would be added to the calendar (June 19). While these and a few other revisions to the Book of Common Prayer were being made, Archbishop Richard Bancroft (now best known for overseeing the production of the King James Version of the Bible) slipped into the calendar Saint Enurchus, Bishop of Orléans. Who is Enurchus? It was a misprint of *Evurtius*, an obscure French bishop from the 300s. (This misprint would be retained for almost three hundred years in printings of the prayer book.) There is no particular reason for Bancroft to include Evurtius in the calendar—except one. His name starts with *E*, and he died on September 7, which just happens to be . . . the birthday of Queen Elizabeth I.

The other day not in the medieval calendar was a commemoration added in 1662: the Venerable Bede, Presbyter (May 27). Bede, a monk in the far north of England, died in 735. Before the century was out, his monastery would be sacked by Vikings, but he lived a life of holiness and peace. He was the first great English historian, as well as an avid biblical commentator, translator, poet, and observer of the natural world. In his time, Bede was widely regarded as the most learned man in the British Isles, and one of the most learned in Europe.[9]

What if you want to remember with thanksgiving the life of one of these saints with black-letter days? Or other faithful Christians, whether from the early centuries of the church like Saint Monica and Saint Athanasius, or reformers like Martin Luther and Archbishop Thomas Cranmer, or missionaries and translators like Henry Martyn and Bishop Samuel Ajayi Crowther, or the Martyrs of Uganda and the Martyrs of Papua New Guinea? Prayers for this purpose are on pages 711-713 and page 716. May God "give us grace so to follow their good examples, that with them we may be partakers" of his "heavenly kingdom" (p. 251).

At a Glance: Examples of How the Collects for Saints' Days Changed at the Reformation

	Medieval collect (Sarum): translation from Latin	*Prayer Book collect (1662 IE)*
St. Thomas	Grant us, Lord, we beseech thee, so to rejoice in the anniversary of thy blessed apostle Thomas, that we may ever be assisted by his protection and eagerly follow the example of his faith with fitting devotion. Through, etc.	Almighty and ever-living God, who for the greater confirmation of the faith didst suffer thy holy apostle Thomas to be doubtful of thy Son's resurrection: Grant us so perfectly, and without all doubt, to believe in thy Son Jesus Christ, that our faith in thy sight may never be reproved. Hear us, O Lord, through, etc.
The Annunciation	O God, who didst will that thy Word should take our flesh from the womb of the blessed Virgin Mary at the annunciation of an angel, grant unto us, thy suppliants, that we, who believe her to be truly the mother of God, may be assisted by her intercessions with thee. Through, etc.	We beseech thee, O Lord, pour thy grace into our hearts, that as we have known the incarnation of thy Son Jesus Christ by the message of an angel, so by his cross and passion we may be brought unto the glory of his resurrection, through, etc.

St. Barnabas   O Lord, we beseech thee, let the prayer of thy blessed apostle Barnabas commend thy church to thee, and may he appear as an intercessor for her whom he enlighteneth by his teaching and suffering. Through, etc.

O Lord God almighty, who didst endue thy holy apostle Barnabas with singular gifts of the Holy Ghost: Leave us not, we beseech thee, destitute of thy manifold gifts, nor yet of grace to use them alway to thy honour and glory, through, etc.

10

Where Do I Go From Here?

✠

The Book of Common Prayer offers a well of Christian devotion to which you can return daily for the rest of your life. You never need to move on or leave it behind. But what should you do if you want to drink more deeply from this well?

First, find other people to pray with. You can read Morning and Evening Prayer by yourself, but they're meant to be read with other people. Better yet, find a church that uses the Book of Common Prayer. Then you can pray with a congregation, hear the Scriptures, sing hymns, hear sermons, and regularly partake of Holy Communion. The Book of Common Prayer is designed to connect you with other Christians in a church.

It's easier in some places than others to find classically Anglican worship. The Anglican tradition is like a grand country house; inside there are big fireplaces, cozy corners, and floors made out of ancient oaks and elms. But some of the recent remodeling has been less than ideal (in our view), and the rich wooden floors were covered over with linoleum and orange shag carpet. In many places, there has been a loss of Morning Prayer in public worship, and along with it a loss of the full diet of the Psalms, lengthy narratives from the Old Testament, the *Te Deum*, and the creation themes in the *Benedicite*. The historic eucharistic lectionary, which was in large measure common throughout the Western church for a millennium, is often displaced. And characteristic ways the Book of Common Prayer teaches and forms our spiritual life are sometimes forgotten: from the weekly recitation of the Ten Commandments to a Communion service structured for heavenly ascent. What replaces the classic Book of Common Prayer in some churches can also be very good and edifying, but because the options in late-modern prayer books are so vast, what is done in one place will often not be done in another. So there's no telling exactly what you will find in any particular church.

Besides finding a church, what if you want to learn more about the Book of Common Prayer and the Anglican tradition? This volume is only a short guidebook, and there are many other resources. Here's a road map to help you get started.

Further Reading

The Book of Common Prayer has other services that we haven't discussed. If you want to learn about these, there are many good sources, and the place to start is with a commentary on the 1662 Book of Common Prayer. A recent commentary is Gerald Bray's *A Companion to the Book of Common Prayer*, and another one by Samuel Fornecker and Drew Nathaniel Keane is in preparation (forthcoming 2025). Among older commentaries, three are standouts. Two are from the early twentieth century: Evan Daniel's *The Prayer-Book: Its History, Language, and Contents* and Charles Neil and J. M. Willoughby's *The Tutorial Prayer Book*. Both have a rich supply of information about every part of the prayer book, though their historical scholarship has sometimes been superseded. Thomas Comber's *Companion to the Temple and Closet*, from the 1670s, is seven volumes! It's wordy by today's standards, but is filled with devotional treasures. All three of these older commentaries are out of print but are available free online. Also very useful—if you can work your way through the demanding prose—is Book V of Richard Hooker's celebrated *Of the Laws of Ecclesiastical Polity*, which addresses many elements of prayer book worship and uncovers their theological rationale.

And there are good guides to parts of the Book of Common Prayer. To learn more about the structure of the Communion service, read Gavin Dunbar's essay "Like Eagles in This Life: A Theological Reflection on 'The Order for the Administration of the Lord's Supper or Holy Communion' in the Prayer Books of 1559 and 1662," which is included in a collection of essays called *The Book of Common Prayer: Past, Present, and Future*. An excellent overview of the baptism services is Bishop Stephen W. Sykes's essay

"'Baptisme doth represente unto us oure profession'" in *Thomas Cranmer: Essays in Commemoration of the 500th Anniversary of His Birth*. On the collects, a useful introduction is *The Collects of Thomas Cranmer* by Paul F. M. Zahl and C. Frederick Barbee. It includes each collect, a brief explanation of where it came from, and a devotional application. To learn more about the historical background of the readings, a starting point is David Phillips's essay "The Lectionaries in the Book of Common Prayer," also included in *The Book of Common Prayer: Past, Present, and Future*.

For an introductory history of the prayer book, read Alan Jacobs's *The Book of Common Prayer: A Biography*. While it occasionally relies on outdated historical accounts of the English Reformation,[1] Jacobs's history really shines in his exquisite description of the prayer book's text and its spiritual impact on generations of people using it.

The classic Book of Common Prayer uses older language, and the reasons for this were sketched in chapter one. If you want to go further on language and worship, start with C. S. Lewis's essay called "'Miserable Offenders': An Interpretation of Prayer Book Language," which is reprinted in *God in the Dock: Essays on Theology and Ethics*. Then, to read about how churches over the past two millennia have worshiped using a distinct "voice" that differs from ordinary speech, see Gerald Bonner's chapter in *Thomas Cranmer: Essays in Commemoration of the 500th Anniversary of His Birth* called "Liturgical Language and Devotion." If you want to go still further, an incomparably comprehensive analysis is Stella Brook's *The Language of the Book of Common*

Prayer (available free from Internet Archive). On the related question about why the prayer book liturgies are fixed texts, and not flexible shapes, see Samuel L. Bray, "The Shape Fallacy: The Book of Common Prayer as Text," published in *Ad Fontes* (March 2020) and republished in *Faith & Worship* (Trinity 2020).

Music and the Book of Common Prayer have gone together from the beginning. Two common ways of singing the canticles and psalms are Anglican Chant, which is a harmonized melody; and plainsong, which is a unison melody. You have probably noticed that some of the text in the Book of Common Prayer is printed with an asterisk near the middle of each line; the asterisk is meant to guide the chanting, showing when to move to the next part of the melody. Basic resources for learning how to chant can be found in *The Hymnal 1940* of the Episcopal Church; *The New English Hymnal: Melody Edition*; and the 2017 hymnal of the Reformed Episcopal Church (printed under two names, *The Book of Common Praise* and *Magnify the Lord*).

The Book of Common Prayer is not the only defining text, or "formulary," of the Anglican tradition. Another is the Anglican confessional statement, the Articles of Religion. A recent treatment of the Articles can be found in Gerald Bray's book *Anglicanism: A Reformed Catholic Tradition*. One weakness is that Bray's book tends to play down the doctrinal authority of the prayer book, especially on baptism, but on most points he offers a knowledgeable yet still brisk and readable introduction. More comprehensive is Bishop Edward Harold Browne's classic work from the mid-1800s called *An Exposition of the Thirty-Nine Articles: Historical and Doctrinal.* Browne demonstrates how each of the Articles is supported by the Scriptures and the church fathers, and though some of his scholarship is dated now, most of it holds up.

The two Books of Homilies are official expositions of the doctrine of the church. These date to the reigns of Edward VI and Elizabeth I, and they were designed to ensure sound preaching throughout England. In his "Directions for Preaching," King James I of England (VI of Scotland) called them "a pattern and a boundary, as it were, for the preaching ministry."[2] Both Books of Homilies are endorsed by the Articles of Religion, which say they "contain a godly and wholesome doctrine and necessary for these times" (Article 35, p. 642). One of the homilies is included as an appendix in the 1662 International Edition (p. 654). To read more of the homilies, an accessible starting point is Lee Gatiss's modernization of the first Book called *The First Book of Homilies: The Church of England's Official Sermons in Modern English.* An older printing of both Books of Homilies is available free online: *The Two Books of Homilies Appointed to Be Read in Churches,* edited by John Griffiths.

Finally, the Book of Common Prayer has the fingerprints of Archbishop Thomas Cranmer on every page. Do you want to learn more about this man, who was a Cambridge don, then an unlikely archbishop, and finally a Reformation martyr? The unsurpassed biography is by Diarmaid Mac-Culloch, *Thomas Cranmer: A Life.*

Notes

1 LITURGY?

[1]Gerald Bray, *A Companion to the Book of Common Prayer* (Cambridge: James Clarke & Co., 2023), 322.

[2]Alan Jacobs, *The Book of Common Prayer: A Biography* (Princeton, NJ: Princeton University Press, 2013), 105-6.

[3]C. S. Lewis, "To Mary Van Deusen," April 1, 1952, *The Collected Letters of C. S. Lewis: Narnia, Cambridge, and Joy 1950-1963*, edited by Walter Hooper, vol. 3 (San Francisco: HarperCollins, 2007), 177-78.

[4]Annie Dillard, *Holy the Firm* (New York: Harper & Row, 1988), 59.

[5]C. S. Lewis, *Letters to Malcolm: Chiefly on Prayer* (New York: Harcourt, Brace & World, 1963), 6.

[6]Compare D. E. W. Harrison, *Common Prayer in the Church of England* (London: SPCK, 1969), 119-20: "The preached word may vary according to the doctrinal idiosyncrasies of the preacher; extempore prayer, both in its range and in its depth, is similarly conditioned, but a liturgy which is itself sound is a bastion against both false and shallow doctrine."

[7]Compare Aidan Kavanagh, *Elements of Rite: A Handbook of Liturgical Style* (New York: Pueblo Publishing, 1982), 28: "*Repetition and rhythm*

169

in the liturgy are to be fostered. No rule is more frequently violated by the highly educated and well-meaning, who seem to think that never having to repeat anything is a mark of effective communication."

[8]C. K. Barrett, *A Critical and Exegetical Commentary on the Acts of the Apostles* (Edinburgh: T&T Clark, 1994), 166.

[9]See Jonathan Gibson and Mark Earngey, *Reformation Worship: Liturgies from the Past for the Present* (Greensboro, NC: New Growth Press, 2018).

[10]Compare Judith Maltby, *Prayer Book and People in Elizabethan and Early Stuart England* (Cambridge: Cambridge University Press, 1998), 233: "Familiarity does not always breed contempt; it may nurture devotion."

[11]See Charles Simeon, *Horae Homileticae*, vol. 2 (London: Holdworth and Ball, 1832), 249: "What are hymns, but forms of prayer and praise? and if it be lawful to worship God in forms of verse, is it not equally so in forms of prose?"

2 A Ten-Minute History of the Prayer Book

[1]Brian Cummings, *The Book of Common Prayer: A Very Short Introduction* (Oxford: Oxford University Press, 2018), 1.

[2]Margaret Anne Doody, "Jane Austen's Reading," in *The Jane Austen Companion*, edited by J. David Grey (New York: Macmillan, 1986), 347.

[3]Alan Jacobs, *The Book of Common Prayer: A Biography* (Princeton, NJ: Princeton University Press, 2013), 193-94.

[4]Paul Dyck, "George Herbert and the Liturgical Experience of Scripture," in *George Herbert's Pastoral: New Essays on the Poet and Priest of Bemerton*, edited by Christopher Hodgkins (Newark: University of Delaware Press, 2010), 199.

[5]G. J. Cuming, *A History of Anglican Liturgy*, 2nd edition (Houndmills, Basingstoke, Hampshire and London: Macmillan Press, 1982), 127. See also Charles Hefling, "The 'Liturgy of Comprehension,'" in *The Oxford Guide to the Book of Common Prayer: A Worldwide Survey*, edited by Charles Hefling and Cynthia Shattuck (New York: Oxford University Press, 2006), 61: "The Prayer Book restored to use in 1662 was to all intents the same as the one restored at the beginning of Queen Elizabeth's reign. Many small improvements had been made, but none was of much doctrinal significance."

[6]*Episcopal*, as applied to a church, means "governed by bishops." It is from *episkopos*, a Greek word for "guardian, overseer" adopted by early Christians for the leaders of their communities. That is also where we get the term *episcopalian*, which refers to one who belongs to an episcopal church or who advocates for rule by bishops. The English word *bishop* is an Anglo-Saxon truncation of the Greek.

[7]J. I. Packer, "The Status of the Articles," in *The Articles of the Church of England*, edited by H. E. W. Turner (Oxford: Mowbray, 1964), 48.

[8]See, for example, Esther Mombo, "Anglican Liturgies in Eastern Africa," in *The Oxford Guide to the Book of Common Prayer*, 277.

[9]Canons of the Church of England, A5 ("In particular, [the church's] doctrine is to be grounded in the Thirty-Nine Articles of Religion, *The Book of Common Prayer*, and the Ordinal."); Global South Fellowship of Anglican Churches, Covenantal Structure, 1.1 (same); Principles of Canon Law Common to the Churches of the Anglican Communion (2008), nos. 55.1 ("The Book of Common Prayer 1662 is the normative standard for liturgy.") and 55.6 ("Liturgical adaptation and innovation must not be inconsistent with the Word of God and with the spirit and teaching of the Book of Common Prayer 1662."); J. Robert Wright, "The Book of Common Prayer," in *The Wiley-Blackwell Companion to the Anglican Communion*, edited by Ian S. Markham et al. (Oxford: Wiley-Blackwell, 2013), 83 ("[T]he 1662 revision of the English prayer book is widely recognized as being authoritative for the worldwide Anglican Communion today.").

3 THE ASCENT OF MORNING AND EVENING PRAYER

[1]C. S. Lewis, "'Miserable Offenders': An Interpretation of Prayer Book Language," *in God in the Dock: Essays on Theology and Ethics*, edited by Walter Hooper (Grand Rapids, MI: Eerdmans Publishing, 2014), 123.

[2]This view—that in the absence of a priest, the absolution in Morning and Evening Prayer can be read even by a layman or laywoman—was the position of the first commentator on the Book of Common Prayer, John Boys, who was the dean of Canterbury Cathedral (1619–1625). See John Boys, *The Ministers Invitatorie in The Workes of John Boys* (London: Aspley, 1629), 305. Compare J. I. Packer, Interview with Julie Lane-Gay, *Anglican Studies Program* (undated): "When you are saying the Office

on your own, you become the leader. Then, I believe, you can properly say everything, including the absolution, to yourself and indeed need to."

[3]A. Theodore Wirgman, *The Prayer Book with Scriptural Proofs and Historical Notes* (London: Bemrose & Sons, 1873), 25, quoting Mark 9:24.

[4]J. Chester Johnson, *Auden, The Psalms, and Me* (New York: Church Publishing, 2017), 89.

[5]C. S. Lewis, *Reflections on the Psalms* (San Francisco: HarperCollins, 2017), 7.

[6]Ernest Clapton, *Our Prayer Book Psalter: Containing Coverdale's Version from His 1535 Bible and the Prayer Book Version by Coverdale from the Great Bible, 1539-41, Printed Side by Side* (London: Society for Promoting Christian Knowledge, 1934), 49-50.

[7]Athanasius, "Letter of St. Athanasius to Marcellinus on the Interpretation of the Psalms," in St. Athanasius, *On the Incarnation: The Treatise De Incarnatione Verbi Dei*, translated and edited by a religious of the C.S.M.V. (Crestwood, NY: Saint Vladimir's Seminary Press, 1953), 103.

[8]Richard Hooker, *Of the Laws of Ecclesiastical Polity*, edited by W. Speed Hill, vol. 2, *The Folger Library Edition of The Works of Richard Hooker* (Cambridge, MA: The Belknap Press of Harvard University Press, 1977), book V, chapter 37.1.

[9]Gordon Wenham, *Psalms as Torah: Reading Biblical Song Ethically* (Grand Rapids, MI: Baker Academic, 2012), chapter 4.

[10]"A Fruitful Exhortation to the Reading and Knowledge of Holy Scripture," in *The Two Books of Homilies Appointed to Be Read in Churches*, edited by John Griffiths (Oxford: Oxford University Press, 1859), 15.

[11]On this point of continuity with the medieval offices, see Jesse D. Billett, "A Spirituality of the Word: The Medieval Roots of Traditional Anglican Worship," *Pro Ecclesia*, vol. 27, no. 2, 157-179 (2018), 173: "In the Divine Office, the scriptures are always answered with praise: every lesson from scripture is made an occasion for thanksgiving. And it is only in that setting that scripture can be understood correctly."

[12]Thomas Comber, *Companion to the Temple: or, a Help to Devotion in the Daily Use of the Common Prayer*, vol 1., 3rd edition (London: Printed by M. Clark for Henry Brome, 1679), 339.

[13]Janel M. Mueller, *The Native Tongue and the Word: Developments in English Prose Style 1380–1580* (Chicago: The University of Chicago Press, 1984), 243. "Functionally and formally the collect is well named, whether one chooses to trace its inception to Latin *collectio* (a summation offered by the priest to draw together the various inward responses of the people to the biddings enjoined on them in the liturgy) or to Latin *collecta*, short for *oratio ad collectam* (a prayer said over the gathered people, and hence one that speaks for them all as a group)." Mueller, *The Native Tongue*, 227.

[14]Martin Parsons, *The Holy Communion: An Exposition of the Prayer Book Service* (London: Hodder and Stoughton, 1961), 42. See also James A. Devereux, S.J., "Reformed Doctrine in the Collects of the First Book of Common Prayer," *The Harvard Theological Review*, vol. 58, no. 1, 49-68 (1965), 50 (noting that ancient Latin collects translated for the Book of Common Prayer "clearly reflect an orthodox insistence on the absolute preeminence of God's grace, and the helplessness of man to do anything without Him").

4 Further Up and Further In

[1]Martin Davie, *Our Inheritance of Faith: A Commentary on the Thirty-Nine Articles* (Malton, North Yorkshire: Gilead Books, 2019), 294. Compare J. N. D. Kelly, *The Athanasian Creed* (London: A. and C. Black, 1964), 125-26 ("So far from suggesting that Christian faith is no more than intellectual assent, [the Athanasian Creed] starts off by affirming that it consists in *worshipping* the divine Trinity.").

[2]John Boys, *The Ministers Invitatorie in The Workes of John Boys* (London: Aspley, 1629), 45.

[3]J. I. Packer, *The Gospel in the Prayer Book* (Appleford, UK: Marcham Manor Press, 1966. Reprint, Downers Grove, IL: IVP Academic, 2021), omissions not marked.

[4]László Dobszay, *The Restoration and Organic Development of the Roman Rite*, edited and introduced by Laurence Paul Hemming (London: T&T Clark, 2010), 130.

[5]The law of the Church of England required ordination of new ministers to be on the Sundays after the Ember Weeks. Canons of 1604, no. 31.

5 THE ASCENT CONTINUES: BAPTISM AND CONFIRMATION

[1]"An Homily Wherein Is Declared that Common Prayer and Sacraments Ought to Be Ministered in a Tongue that Is Understood of the Hearers," in *The Two Books of Homilies Appointed to Be Read in Churches*, edited by John Griffiths (Oxford: Oxford University Press, 1859), 352.

[2]See, for example, Joachim Jeremias, *Infant Baptism in the First Four Centuries* (London: SCM, 1960).

[3]Canons of 1604, no. 30. Canon 30 gives several reasons for retaining the sign of the cross in baptism, and they have been helpfully summarized this way:

1. Despite the abuse of the sign by the medieval Church, its original purpose was good. The abuse of a thing does not mean that the thing itself should be abolished.

2. The sign of the cross is not part of the baptismal service itself, which is valid without it.

3. The baptised person is received into the Church by baptism, not by the sign of the cross, which is merely an external confirmation of that.

4. It is always good and right to remember that the Cross is central to our faith and that the Christian is called to spiritual warfare under its banner.

Gerald Bray, *A Companion to the Book of Common Prayer* (Cambridge: James Clarke & Co., 2023), 374.

[4]Compare Kenneth Stevenson, "Richard Hooker and the Lord's Prayer: a chapter in Reformation controversy," *Scottish Journal of Theology*, vol. 57, no. 1, 39-55 (2004): 51 (noting that in medieval services and in the Book of Common Prayer the Lord's Prayer is used both "as an introduction and preparation, and then as part of the central core of prayer at the end").

[5]*Catechism of the Catholic Church*, 2nd edition (New York: Doubleday, 2003), 319, ¶ 1128, though also teaching that "the fruits" of baptism depend on the individual's disposition.

[6]Richard Hooker, *Of the Laws of Ecclesiastical Polity*, edited by W. Speed Hill, vol. 2, *The Folger Library Edition of The Works of Richard Hooker*

(Cambridge, MA: The Belknap Press of Harvard University Press, 1977), book V, chapter 64.2.

[7]Martin Luther, *The Babylonian Captivity of the Church*, in *The Annotated Luther: Church and Sacraments*, edited by Paul W. Robinson et al., vol. 3 (Minneapolis: Fortress Press, 2016), 63.

[8]James Ussher, *A Body of Divinity, or The Sum and Substance of Christian Religion Catechistically Propounded, and Explained, by Way of Question and Answer, Methodically and Familiarly Handled* (London: printed for Nath. Ranew and J. Robinson, at the Kings Arms in St. Pauls Churchyard, 1670), 417.

[9]Alexander Nowell wrote two catechisms. The more widely used one, called the "Middle Catechism," was written in Latin and then translated into English. It was officially authorized by the Church of England as a companion to the prayer book catechism, and church law required its use in schools. Canons of 1604, no. 79. The high regard for Nowell's Middle Catechism can be seen from a sermon by John Donne, who praised it and the prayer book catechism this way: "all that doctrine which wrought this great cure upon us, in the Reformation, is contained in the two catechisms, in the Thirty-Nine Articles, and in the two Books of Homilies." John Donne, "Sermon CLV: Preached at St. Paul's Cross, September 14, 1622," in *The Works of John Donne, D.D.*, vol. 6 (London: John W. Parker, 1839), 215.

6 Ascending to Heaven: Holy Communion

[1]Lyle D. Bierma, *The Theology of the Heidelberg Catechism: A Reformation Synthesis* (Louisville, KY: Westminster John Knox Press, 2013), 167.

[2]John Jewel, *Two Treatises: I. On the Holy Scriptures. II. On the Sacraments* (Oxford: J. H. Parker, 1840), 175-76.

[3]Thomas Cranmer, *A Defense of the True and Catholick Doctrine and Use of the Sacrament of the Body and Blood of Our Saviour Christ*, edited by Henry John Todd (London: C. and J. Rivington, 1825), 26. See also Jewel, *Two Treatises*, 106: "In the word we have his promises; in the sacraments we see them"; John Boys, *An Exposition of the Dominicall Epistles and Gospels used in our English Liturgie, throughout the whole yeere*, in *The Workes of John Boys* (London: Aspley, 1629), 837: "His word is an audible sacrament and his sacraments are visible words."

[4]Samuel L. Bray and John F. Hobbins, *Genesis 1-11: A New Old Translation for Readers, Scholars, and Translators* (Wilmore, KY: GlossaHouse, 2017), 135-38.

[5]Katie Badie, "The Prayer of Humble Access," *Churchman* 120, no. 2, 103-17 (2006): 113.

[6]As one of the official homilies puts it, in this "heavenly Supper . . . every one of us must be guests and not gazers, eaters and not lookers, feeding ourselves and not hiring others to feed for us." "An Homily of the Worthy Receiving and Reverent Esteeming of the Sacrament of the Body and Blood of Christ," in *The Two Books of Homilies Appointed to Be Read in Churches*, edited by John Griffiths (Oxford: Oxford University Press, 1859), 439.

[7]Jewel, *Two Treatises*, 176-77.

7 Reading the Bible with the Prayer Book

[1]Ernest Gordon Rupp, *Six Makers of English Religion 1500–1700* (London: Hodder and Stoughton, 1957), 43.

[2]Samuel L. Bray, "A Neglected Gem: The Sunday First Lessons in the 1662 Book of Common Prayer," *Covenant*, December 11, 2018.

8 The Prayer Book and the Christian Year

[1]John Davenant, *An Exposition of the Epistle of St. Paul to the Colossians*, vol. 1 (London: Hamilton, Adams, and Co., 1831), 485.

[2]Davenant, *An Exposition*, 485, quoting *The City of God*, book 10. Compare Richard Paquier, *Dynamics of Worship: Foundations and uses of liturgy*, translated by Donald Macleod (Philadelphia: Fortress Press, 1967), 104: "Just as in the natural order the old earthly creation makes a tour each year around the physical sun, so in the order of grace, the church—the first fruit of the new creation—makes a cycle each year around its spiritual Sun, Christ, in order to experience successively all its beams and to contemplate the various aspects of it."

[3]George Herbert, "Ungratefulness," in *The Complete English Works*, edited and introduced by Ann Pasternak Slater (New York: Alfred A. Knopf, 1995), 79.

[4]See Thomas J. Talley, *The Origins of the Liturgical Year*, 2nd emended edition (Collegeville, MN: Liturgical Press, 1986), 79-155, especially 91-99, 153-54.

[5]For analysis of the Commination homily, see Liam Beadle, "No Imposition: The Commination and Lent," *Faith & Worship*, no. 82, 16-30 (Lent 2018): 21-22; Samuel L. Bray, "Ashes in a Time of Plague," *Faith & Worship*, no. 88, 48-64 (Lent 2021): 53-55.

[6]George Herbert, "Lent," in *The Complete English Works*, 84-85.

[7]"An Homily for the Days of Rogation Week," in *The Two Books of Homilies Appointed to Be Read in Churches*, edited by John Griffiths (Oxford: Oxford University Press, 1859), 484.

[8]Augustine, "Sermon 271," in *Sermons III/7 (230-272B): On Liturgical Seasons*, translated and with notes by Edmund Hill, O.P., edited by John E. Rotelle, O.S.A. *The Works of Saint Augustine: A Translation for the 21st Century* (Hyde Park, NY: New City Press, 1993), 295.

[9]Anthony Sparrow, *A Rationale upon the Book of Common Prayer of the Church of England* (London: printed for Blanche Pawlet, at the Sign of the Bible in Chancery-Lane, near Fleet-Street, [1684] 1839), 168.

9 THE COMMUNION OF SAINTS

[1]Augustine, "Sermon 76," in *Sermons III (51-94): On the New Testament*, translated and with notes by Edmund Hill, O.P., edited by John E. Rotelle, O.S.A., *The Works of Saint Augustine: A Translation for the 21st Century* (Brooklyn, NY: New City Press, 1991), 311.

[2]Augustine, "Sermon 76," 313.

[3]"An Homily Against Peril of Idolatry and Superfluous Decking of Churches," in *The Two Books of Homilies Appointed to Be Read in Churches*, edited by John Griffiths (Oxford: Oxford University Press, 1859), 227.

[4]Edward T. Horn III, *The Christian Year* (Philadelphia: Muhlenberg Press, 1957), 183.

[5]J. Robert Wright, *Readings from the Daily Office for the Early Church* (New York: Church Publishing, 1991), 459.

[6]The red-letter day immediately after the Conversion of Saint Paul is the Presentation of Christ in the Temple (February 2), which is discussed in chapter eight.

[7]John Donne, "Upon the Annunciation and Passion Falling Upon One Day" in *Selected Poetry*, edited by John Carey (Oxford: Oxford University Press, 1996), 186-87.

[8]Edward Meyrick Goulburn, *The Collects of the Day: An Exposition Critical and Devotional of the Collects Appointed at the Communion*, vol. 2 (New York: E. & J. B. Young, 1883), 372.

[9]J. Campbell, "Bede [St Bede, Bæda, *known as* the Venerable Bede] (673/4–735)," in *Oxford Dictionary of National Biography*, edited by H. C. G. Matthew and Brian Harrison, vol. 4 (Oxford: Oxford University Press, 2004), 764-65: "Recognition of Bede's qualities has flourished since his own day. Boniface wrote that he shone like a candle of the church by his knowledge of the scriptures (Monumenta Germaniae Historica, Epistolae Selectae, 1, 1916, no. 76)."

10 WHERE DO I GO FROM HERE?

[1]For more current accounts, see the chapters in *The Oxford History of Anglicanism, Volume I: Reformation and Identity, c.1520–1662*, edited by Anthony Milton (Oxford: Oxford University Press, 2017).

[2]Anthony Milton, *England's Second Reformation: The Battle for the Church of England, 1625–1662* (Cambridge: Cambridge University Press, 2021), 44.

General Index

Anglican Formularies
Index